TRANSFYOUR *Life*

by

Darren Harris

Linda Gentilcore

Cynthia Cavalli, Ph.D.

Sarah Patrick

Sera Johnston

James Woodworth

Deepti G Gujar

Dr. Jerry D. Smith Jr.

Ruth Owen

Brian Peters

Joana Visa, Ph.D.

Sai Blackbyrn

Transforming Your Life

Sai Blackbyn

With

Co-Authors from around the World

Transforming Your Life

All Rights Reserved

Copyright 2018

Transforming Your Life

sai@sai.coach

Sai Blackbyn

Transforming Your Life

ISBN 978-1-5272-2922-8

Edited by Surbhi Sanchali Gupta
Interior Design by Jeanly Fresh Zamora
Project Management by Antonetta Fernandes

Darren Harris
2 Time Blind Paralympian, Change Agent

Linda Gentilcore
Human Resources Veteran, Leadership Guru

Cynthia Cavalli, Ph.D.
Aerospace Engineer, Synchronicity Coach

Sarah Patrick
Remedy Maker and Transformation Coach

Sera Johnston
Master coach, trainer, author, and mentor

James Woodworth
Teacher, Trainer, Coach, and Mentor

Deepti G Gujar
Inner Child work and Rebirthing Breathwork Coach

Dr. Jerry D. Smith Jr.
Clinical Psychologist, Business Consultant,
and Leadership Development Coach

Ruth Owen
Journalist, Baker, Speaker, Coach

Brian Peters
World Champion Athlete, Market-Leading Sales Coach, Mentor, Author

Joana Visa, Ph.D.
Coach and mentor with scientific background

Sai Blackbyrn
CEO, Mentor, Speaker, Coach for Coaches

Foreword by Mynoo Maryel
founder of The PoEM foundation
and Best-Selling Author of The BE Book

This book is dedicated to all those seeking
transformational change

Foreword

M Y N O O   M A R Y E L

founder of The PoEM foundation and Best-Selling Author of The BE Book

To: The Readers of the Transforming Your Life Series

"In writing this foreword I am reminded of the famous Bob Dylan song "Times they are a changing..." written in 1954. This was an emerging reality then and now we are in an era where change is constant, uncertainty is certain, chaos is consistent, sustainability is unsustainable, continuous evolution is the new performance metric.

We are moving away from the age where survival of the fittest was the norm. Thus, we are creating a "win/lose" environment, where competition and winning at all costs have become the dogged pursuit, the era where "Greed is good".

We have entered a realm where collaboration, co-creation and interdependence is the reality. Ability to cooperate is the new competitive advantage. An era where trust is the new brand, good is good, openness is the new focus, and adaptability is the key to consistency. Spirituality is the next big thing.

Slow is the new fast. Fast food is unhealthy and slow food provides greater nourishment, and this can be applied to capital too. A shift from venture capital to nurture capital. Business for the good is proving to be good for business, as evidenced by the success of Mastercard, Virgin and several new business models emerging around the world.

"Times indeed are a changing…" We live and work in extraordinary times and they require extraordinary leadership and result in us living extraordinary lives where all aspects of our life coexist with ease, grace and joy.

In some areas, this will require a radical reinvention. This is often not doable or even feasible. Transformation is the call of the moment. How can you prepare for this? What can you practically do? What resources, tools, tricks and practices are available to support you along the way?

"Transforming your life" provides many answers that can support and navigate you as you go through the turbulence, joys, challenges and excitement of living, while working and leveraging the opportunities in these times.

Each author takes you through their best insider secrets and you learnt from their journey of uncovering these and working with them as they transform their lives. This book is rich in juicy nuggets, insights and inspirations; from leaders who have "been there and done that". Each one adorns the scars as well as the medals and shares generously what supported them, to transform themselves.

This book can be read from start to finish or you open up at any page and read the chapter that that page is a part of. Synchronistically, you will find it both relevant and appropriate to the answers you are seeking at that point in time.

Finally, remember, its great to have a light bulb AHA moment. What makes the difference is the implementation. So, make your choice to implement consistently and enjoy the journey along the way.

What you have with you is a practical guidebook and to benefit from its rewards, make it your workbook. Enjoy the successes, experience the fulfilment and share in the abundance, as you achieve unprecedented results whilst also transforming your own quality of life, that of others and the planet itself."

TABLE OF CONTENTS

Break Through the
Prison of Your Mind

SERA JOHNSTON

With the impending arrival of our first child, our thoughts turned to the future. We were imagining life with our daughter. Who will she resemble? What will her characteristics be like? What will interest her—ballet, dance or sports? I know only one thing for sure. I'll be on maternity leave for the whole year, so I can spend those precious months caring for her and watching every development. After a year, I would return to work and continue my career while my in-laws care for my daughter. Three days after the predicted due date, Dana Amelia was born, 7lbs 6oz. Finally, two weeks after giving birth by emergency caesarean, we were given the all clear to go home. I can't quite believe that after all this time we can begin our life as a new family. The picture I had of our new family since the pregnancy was far from reality and something I was not prepared for.

The car turns the corner, and I can see our house. We are home at last. I feel scared because there are no nurses to call upon for help now. What if I can't do this? Be a mum, that is. What if I don't know what to do? My mind wonders yet again. As Dana is carried in her car seat through the front door for the very first time, I whisper

"Welcome to your home, Dana." It feels good to be home. This is it; we are on our own. We can start being a family and look forward to a wonderful life.

The nursery is already furnished: changing mat on the chest of drawers, a Winnie the Pooh toy over the cot, nappies and toiletries lined on the shelves, and pictures of Disney characters on the colourful walls. I soon develop a daily routine. Once we were both fed and dressed in the mornings, would either go for a walk or attend a mother-and-baby group. I am thrown into conversations about babies' sleeping and feeding habits. It almost feels like a contest between these little babies, between mothers who follow their own methods, and others who follow step-by-step instructions from books. I am both fascinated and intrigued, so I listen with interest. The mother and baby groups become a regular meet up, and the babies soon start to crawl around to explore their environment. Dana and others are not interested, so they sit with us while we chat among ourselves. Some children are late developers, this is a well-known fact. All babies catch up eventually. I was reassured several times by the health visitor, at the weekly check-ins, that there was nothing to worry about. I was told that Dana was healthy and happy. After all, I had the red book—a book that records the weight, height and wellbeing of a baby's development—as a confirmation.

After six weeks, I was able to drive, which gave me much more freedom. Life for us, as a family, became full of joy and precious memories. Celebrating Dana's first birthday with family and friends was magical. Where had the time gone? She was a year old already. As I prepared her for bed, thoughts turned to my forthcoming return to work as a working mum and to establishing a routine. Was I doing the right thing? I was torn between staying at home or going to work, but I knew that going to work was the right thing for me, even though I missed her so much.

One Monday morning, I was sitting nervously, waiting for a home visit from Dana's assigned health visitor. I had received a call a week ago requesting a visit because the doctor herself was returning from maternity leave. As Dana lay on her play mat, with toys surrounding her, the doorbell rang. It was the health visitor. I invited her in, asked if she would like a cup of tea, and we sat down to start chatting. She fell silent and looked at me. I started to feel uncomfortable—What is she going to say? It took her a few moments to compose herself, and she said, "I have concerns about Dana's development, and I recommend that she is seen by a paediatrician."

I had to ask her to repeat herself as I thought I misheard her. What was she saying and why was she saying these things? It couldn't be true! You only had to look at my beautiful baby girl and see that there is nothing wrong as she giggled and smiled playing happily with her toys. The health visitor had got this wrong; she'd mixed Dana up with someone else. I knew this to be true because Dana was seen by a paediatrician before discharge, who gave both of us the all clear. I felt betrayed. I invited her into my home unprepared for the real intention of her visit. I dismissed her words as quickly as I dismissed her out of my home.

With the health visitor's words swirling in my head, I sat in the paediatrician's office, nervously waiting to be called in. Dana was blissfully sitting in her car seat, unaware of how scared I was. My stomach was in knots, and the only thing on my mind at that moment was wanting to run away. I knew that they had made a mistake and that we would sit in the paediatrician's office and laugh. We would be home soon and resume our lives.

"I think your child has Cerebral Palsy, and I would like to do an MRI scan to confirm." Those words shook me to my core. They were given harshly and coldly, without any empathy. Clearly, the paediatrician did not consider the impact that these words would have on us. She just took it in her stride with no emotion. What was happening? The paediatrician has only just met Dana, and she had already formed an opinion. An incorrect one at that.

In just one hour, my hopes and dreams were quashed as the future was now uncertain. I was suddenly entering a new world that was unknown to me and that I had no experience of. A new language was being spoken, and I didn't understand what it meant. With nobody to help and guide me, Google became my best friend. While I was searching what Cerebral Palsy was and how it will impact Dana's life, a part of me still believed that the medics had made a mistake.

I searched for the best paediatricians in Harley Street for a second opinion. Surely, *they* would see on the MRI scan that Dana was fine. Yet again, I was told, "Your child has Cerebral Palsy." I knew from the Google searches that the world will try to pigeonhole my daughter or make her just another statistic. There was no way that I'd let that happen to my child. I made a vow to myself that day: I would do whatever it took to ensure that Dana would lead an independent life. I didn't know how, but I knew that it was my responsibility as her mum to love, care, and protect her at any cost. And so, my Mantra was born: "Get the Job Done."

I explained the diagnosis to my family and friends as best as I could, but how do you really explain something that you yourself do not completely understand. They either took pity or distanced themselves from us. I had just gotten used becoming a first-time mum, going back to work, and becoming a new family. Now, I had another role to play—all without any guidance or support. I became alienated from the mother-and-baby group because Dana was the only child there with a disability. This was my first encounter of the staring and whispering among mothers. I took this personally, and I either became defensive and aggressive or submissive. My only concern was my child. What did they know?

Determined to live by my mantra, returning to work was the one area that I could be myself—or so I thought. I was consumed with the idea of being in control of everything, and I threw myself into my work. I created an alternative persona and convinced those around me that everything was fine. I was doing a good job, and there was no evidence to prove otherwise—except that I was hiding behind a label—my profession. I was hiding the fact that I was lonely, depressed, and filled with guilt, judgment, and a lack of self-worth. I kept thinking that I should be happy as I had a supportive husband and a beautiful daughter, but I felt sad. I was permanently trapped, trapped in my own head. Other mums were getting on with being mums, what was wrong with me? Work was my escape, but not like before. It was different now. I had to prove that I could do it all as a working mum who would bring up a child with a disability.

Weeks turned into months and months into years, but I was still feeling like I was on a hamster wheel. Consumed with hospital appointments, physio sessions, orthotic appointments, equipment shopping, and form filling, it was official. We were in the system. The new jargon of medical, school, and social services was becoming the norm. I was still using the persona I created at work to function from day to day. Consumed with others' negativity, not only was I fighting to obtain support and aid to help my daughter with her disability, I was also fighting against their biases of how Dana's life would be. I was told she would never hold a pen, told she will be wheelchair bound for life. The negativity was endless and at times too much to hear. I consistently challenged their views and said that this would not be Dana. What do they know, with their faces full of pity staring back at me? I will prove that Dana is not just another statistic.

Every outing and holiday had to be planned in detail: from looking at access to planning the actual journey. Nothing was last minute or spontaneous anymore. This confirmed even more how different my world was now, even having a day out was a task. The freedom I had once had was gone. The people stared as we walked with Dana; children's stares I could understand, but adults who stared just made me angry. Confronting so many people, asking why they were starting, all of it made it even more stressful and just reinforced how so very different we were.

Either to my credit or detriment, the word 'can't' was never an option for me when it came to Dana defining her abilities. This was exactly the case when we enrolled her in StageCoach, a performing arts school held at weekends. At just 5 years, she enrolled, walking with her stick. She was the only child with a disability in the whole school. It was at times stressful and heart-breaking when things were physically impossible for her to do, but she gave 100% to the whole exposure in acting and singing. This lead to acting roles at the BBC and nationwide photoshoots. We were all too familiar with the stares from children and parents with any activity that Dana joined, but we got the most stares when she started her Ballet lessons.

Meeting the teacher before joining, and talking about the practicalities of Dana attending, was a prerequisite. I knew the drill by now, yet no amount of hoop jumping will stop me from giving Dana the experiences that any other child may take for granted.

The drive and focus we had towards allowing Dana to show her capabilities came at a price. When we were invited to a rare party, I was with Dana climbing the tall frames in the play area, while other mothers could just sit and chat with each other. I was missing out on these moments with the other mums. Bitterness and resentment were building up in me, and they surfaced at times like these. The price that I had to pay was suppressing my own needs and hiding behind a label. I wanted to lead a 'normal' life. I wanted to be the mum who takes her child to activities because she has interests and hobbies, just like any other child. I wanted Dana to be seen as a child first, not as the girl who is disabled and doesn't do anything.

The impact on my marriage was evident as all my energy was focused on Dana. My marriage was insignificant, and I didn't care. I went through a miscarriage. I was devastated; it proved to me that I was a complete failure at having children. I couldn't even get the most natural thing for any woman right. I was falling deeper into depression. I was anxious, angry, crying, and my head felt as if it was going to explode. I was consumed with guilt. Dana's disability was my fault.

I thought that if only I had delivered her on the due date, she wouldn't be disabled. I blamed myself. I should have been more assertive with the doctors when I arrived at the hospital, but I had had nothing to compare it with. I was in a very dark place and didn't know what to do. At home, I would disappear and sit in my bedroom all alone, negative thoughts swirling in my head, convinced that I was of no use to anyone. Hours would go by; I didn't want to talk or eat. Sometimes, I just stayed curled up in bed fully clothed. My bedroom became my prison, I was confined day and night. The house became alien to me, and life as a family was non-existent. All I wanted to do was end it, and I knew I would never see this through. I needed help. I was crying out for help. The GP diagnosed me with depression and prescribed Prozac and CBT. I agreed to CBT, but I didn't want to take medication All I wanted was to be listened to. This was my first of many visits to the GP.

There was still a job to be done where it concerned Dana, so I suppressed how I was really feeling because it wasn't important to me, and the next few years were consumed with finding alternative treatments. The NHS has a standard format clinical protocol in its treatment plan, but it wasn't enough. I was consistently being bombarded with negative comments about accepting the things as they were and that there was nothing else available. I didn't accept this. I was on a mission.

When Dana was 2, we took her to Hungary; this was the beginning of the 6 years of travel we undertook, where we spent 3–4 months of each year abroad. My employer was supportive, which was a huge comfort, and allowed me to pursue alternative treatments. Our home was filled with equipment, so we could replicate the Hungarian programme. We were determined to do whatever it took to give her the best possible chance of success. When Dana was 13, we came across a new treatment, which was not performed in the UK yet, that had a high success rate.

Despite all the negative comments, and against the advice of medics, we raised £75,000 in 6 months and flew to the USA for a life-changing operation called Selective Dorsal Rhizotomy (SDR) that has changed her life forever. The predicted life that was mapped out to us in the early years has been quashed, and the medics were astonished at the difference. I know I was the instigator and the driving force behind anything new that I came across. The thought of not pursuing these treatments was not an option. I was completely unaware that I was adding further layers into the jobs that needed to be done. I, the person that I was, again hid behind the work for my child. I was already managing the medical appointments, school meetings, the endless amount of paperwork, all on my own. Debating, negotiating, and putting my point across forcefully was draining, both physically and mentally. I also had to juggle work and somehow function every day.

There was a pattern; I was hiding behind the disability/carer label and functioning on pure emotions such as anger, stress, guilt, judgment, negativity, and depression, just to get the job done. At work, I hid behind the alt persona that I had created; I was functioning by being confident, competent, assertive, driven, in control, tough, and knowledgeable in my management role. Yet, on my own, I was vulnerable, scared, and anxious. I was a failure with no self-worth or self-belief. I would make excuses so as to not socialise with work colleagues outside. I didn't know who I was, so how could I show up as me? Mothers who were once in the baby group disappeared from my social circle; I had nothing in common with them anyway. Our children were very different, and as mums, we were in different worlds.

The way I talked to myself each day was very damaging. I was taking on the role of a victim, not that I knew or acknowledged this. I believed that what I was thinking was true. I was trapped. Trapped in my physical environment and trapped in my head. If what I requested was not done when promised or when I expected it, I would get angry and demand that it be done immediately. When I say 'angry', I mean that I would go for the jugular, metaphorically speaking. I was known as a tyrant and a person who is not to be messed with by those who I came in contact with, professionally and personally.

I was hiding behind this label again, and was proud of it. After all, I was confident and in control; that's what I thought. It was me against the world. When I felt the pressure build up and things got to be too much, I would go back to the GP saying the same things: "I feel down all the time, I keep crying and my child is disabled." What I was really saying is "Listen to me. Poor me. I'm dealing with a lot." I would never say that I couldn't cope.

I kept thinking back to those reports in the news, of children being taken away from their parents, and I didn't want that to happen to me. So, I kept quiet. I didn't really know what I expected from the GP, but one thing was consistent. He would sign me off work because stress and depression. At the time it was a relief, but it also reinforced the way I was feeling. No other support was suggested, so after a few weeks I would be back at work and resume the routine.

It was a Monday morning, and I woke up with the usual 6 am alarm. With the thought of my working day and the meetings scheduled in my diary, I pulled back the bed covers and got out of bed. As I stood and started walking, I veered to the right and walked straight into my wardrobe. Correcting myself, I started walking again, grabbed the door to open it… and walked right into the wall. I ignored it, and thinking that I must be hungry, I started to walk down the stairs, but I couldn't. I was walking towards the wall; I couldn't walk in a straight line. My right arm was tingling, and I was feeling disoriented. I called out to my husband for help. I didn't know what was happening, and I was scared. He helped me down the stairs and sat me on the sofa. When it still wasn't any better after a few hours, my husband explained my symptoms to a doctor over the phone.

He told my husband to bring me down to the surgery but to wait until he calls us back after clarifying something. Within minutes the phone rang again, and the GP asked us to come to the surgery. It was nervous, not knowing what was happening. I walked slowly into the consultation room and was asked to take a seat. The GP assured me that he spoke to his colleague because he originally suspected a heart attack. Thankfully this was not the case, but he couldn't give us a conclusive diagnosis. He sent me to see a consultant and other tests were conducted. I was diagnosed with Vestibular Disorder and BBPV.

This felt like déjà vu. Another diagnosis that I knew nothing about, only this time, the consultant was very knowledgeable and reassured me that it was treatable with specialist physiotherapy. Great, I thought; let's get started then. With an appointment booked within weeks, I walk into the treatment room for my first physio session. After an initial assessment, the treatments began. As I lay on the couch, the physio cupped her hands on either side of my head and gently started rotating. I start spinning, the room is flying through the air, and I feel sick. Grabbing onto the bed, I screamed for her to stop; she comforted me by telling me to breathe, and that it will subside shortly. And it did. I was exhausted; I felt like I had been on a rollercoaster at a speed of 200 miles an hour. "I have to repeat it again," she said. Twenty minutes later, I was back in the waiting room, drinking a cup of water, and trying to make sense of what had just happened. Over the next few months, treatments continued until I felt that I was able to manage the symptoms.

Did I miss the signs? Could I have prevented the frightening episode of that morning, if I had noticed more things about myself? Nobody had the answer. I do remember having an episode at work, where I was feeling distant and foggy in my head. Back then, I just thought that I was doing too much, and had brushed it aside. I had been ignoring most things when it came to my own wellbeing because there were so many other things to focus on that were much more important, at least in my head. Little did I know that my body was sending me signs to stop and listen.

My condition did not disappear as we were originally told, and I believe that the root cause of this development was the stress and internal conflict I had placed myself under for years without listening to my body or looking after myself. I knew this to be true because stress and tiredness were the triggers whenever the symptoms reappeared. As a consequence of this condition, as confirmed by my physio, I was left unable to do several things: tolerate crowds, drive long distances, or have people walk behind me. When sitting in a restaurant or coffee shop, I had to find a table with my back to the wall away from loud noises.

It's ironic. History was repeating itself. This condition, again, was forcing me to plan out my days rigorously so as to avoid any situations that may trigger my symptoms. As the condition was not commonly known within the general medical field, I had to turn to Google once again for a better understanding of what it was. Within a few minutes of searching, it was clear that it was much better known in America, where an organisation was set up specifically for this condition. I found the organisation's ties within a Facebook group, so I immediately requested to join the group. Browsing through the posts, I read stories that were either like mine or were much more severe. It made me thankful for the fact that while it was a horrendous condition, I could still function. Over the years my physio became my go-to person as and when my condition flared up. I was taught how to do the technique at home, but I'd rather have had the physio do the treatment. This was a part of my life now, and now I realised that it was something that I would have to accept.

Enough was Enough

I had been on a downward spiral for years; I felt that every part of me was damaged: mentally, emotionally and physically. Looking in the mirror, I saw a face that was tried, unhappy, and had the worries of the world on her shoulders. I wanted to ask so many questions. Who was she? Was this me? What am I doing? Where am I going? The only thing I was sure of was that I didn't want this, and I couldn't continue the way that I was. Enough was enough. I was exhausted having these layers suffocate me.

I wanted to break free, but how would I do it? In my attempt to keep up the appearance at work, I completed a practitioner course in NLP (Neuro-Linguistic Programming). I'd always been interested and fascinated in the subject as it was to do with the mind, yet it also went further. It explored language, communication, and how our thinking determines our results. This was to be my starting point for my personal development. Even though I had only completed the course to complement my professional skills, it ended up having a profound effect on my behaviours and habits. I was learning how my thinking affected every part of me, and I finally understood how to change it. For the first time after many years, I was putting my needs first and learning who I was. There was so much to learn, especially with a follow-up exam at the end of the course. The classroom training burdened my already long days, and it affected my health. I felt disoriented and foggy; I put it down to tiredness again. I was ignoring it yet again because I was enjoying myself while learning, and I was making friends with the course members.

There was a sense of unity, a feeling of belonging. I don't know whether it was because we delved into personal issues and worked on ourselves, or we just had a connection because we had an interest in the course. Who knows; For the first time ever, I was starting to feel good about myself and noticing minor changes in myself. I passed the exam and became qualified. I enrolled straightaway to complete the Master qualification, too, and passed that exam as well.

I was beginning to change my thinking and started looking at situations from different perspectives. The negativity soon disappeared and the skills that I had learned were not only changing my life, they were changing my working life. I was also helping others make changes in themselves. I felt free. I was free from my mind. Situations were now approached with an open mindset, and I asked the right questions to gain a better understanding, rather than approaching forcefully. I automatically stopped taking on the negativity of others when I learned that you can only change your behaviours, not of those around you. This allowed me to step back and accept that it was okay. I could accept that this was their view; it was my choice not to take on their views. I was seeing a different person emerge, so I continued my journey in discovery and transformation. My background is in training and development, and in supporting others in their development—either personally or professionally. Now, it was my time to focus on me and to completely understand how to make the changes that I needed to make.

I felt really confident, but I was still seeing my physio to treat the vestibular. I was getting frustrated now with the slow progress and decided that with my new outlook I can start taking control of my own treatment by reintroducing exercise. I wasn't sure if this was a good idea, but I had read about others who fully endorsed exercise because they had experienced benefits of it with the same condition. Although everyone is different, I decided to start running to see if it would help. It felt so good to put on my running outfit again; it had been so long. I was remembering completing my first 10k run years ago. I smiled to myself. I started slow: alternating running and walking for 20 minutes. I felt proud of myself. I increased the distance gradually, reducing the time, and eventually started running 2–3 miles almost two or three times a week. I felt great, and with the full support of my physio, incorporated gym workouts into my routine. I was exercising 4–5 times a week, and it felt great. This had a knockout effect on my appearance and the clothes that I wore. I was starting to show my confidence and self-belief through my clothes, and that was important to me. I started to enjoy shopping again, now that I was buying clothes reflecting the new me.

Aligning my mind and body connection was having a profound effect on my wellbeing; incorporating meditation into my routine gave me a stillness and clarity in my head that I really needed. I started introducing daily meditations each morning before starting my day. It cleared the chatter in my head, and allowed me to go deep into my inner self and connect with it. It gave me a sense of calmness that stays with me even today. The feeling of being at peace for 20 minutes each morning felt like having 8 hours of deep sleep. I truly believe that meditation and exercise saved my life; it has been, and still is, my ritual to this day.

Today, I am living by my core values and being true to myself; on the way, I am discovering a deeper understanding, a spiritual understanding that lets me live a life of purpose. I am now tuned in to a deeper connection, living by the Law of Attraction, using affirmations and being in flow with my inner self. I've connected into my energy and shifted blocks that have had resistance. I am not driven by my emotions, as I used to be; now my drive stems from a place of calmness. Everything that happens to us, happens for a reason and has a positive intention. I truly feel blessed that I have experienced the challenges and the low points of my life because, without them, I would not be where I am today. It's not what happens to you, it's how you choose to deal with it. You always have a choice. This connection is also related to my relationship with food. It wasn't so much what I ate but how I was eating it. I understood the principles of clean eating and eating the foods that complemented my exercise training plan, but digging deeper, I understood that food is not just something you eat when you're hungry, it has a direct link to our mood, health, and mind.

It can also mask the root cause of challenges or issues that you're facing. For example, if you are feeling bored and instead of addressing the real reason for your boredom, you reach out for food, then you're not hungry. You are using food to mask your boredom. The relationship you have with food can be a toxic one, and it can unconsciously form habits. For example, when you are watching your favourite programme/film on TV, you grab something sugary or grab a bag of crisps. Sound familiar? You may want this food, but I guarantee that this is a response to the habit that you have formed.

Today, I live a life of purpose that is aligned with my core values. I believe that everything that happens, does so for a reason. It either teaches to learn from the results or makes us realise that some things are just meant to be. My thinking, my behaviour, and my approach is the complete opposite of what it used to be. I shy away from confrontation. If I feel uncomfortable, I either walk away or I don't engage in conversation. I will always have the vestibular condition, but it does not define or limit me. It cannot stop me from achieving my goals. It's just that I may just have to make a few adjustments along the way. As for Dana, well, she is 20 years old now and despite the prognosis and biases of the medics and her schools, is at Canterbury University studying Law and living independently away from home.

I have a belief that the only barriers we face are the ones that we put up ourselves, and in turn, are mimicked by our children. I feel privileged as a mum and a coach if combining my purposes in life helped you on your journey. Each of us holds the key to our own life, so there are no excuses for not taking 100% full responsibility for the choices that we make. Each of us has the power to either enrich our lives by living a life of fulfilment and purpose or stay stuck in a disempowering life where others dictate your future. As always, it's your choice. I believe everyone deserves to be the best version of themselves.

I have some tips for you, so you can begin your journey and start living YOUR life.

1. Focus on what you want and NOT what you don't want. Set small goals that are achievable and realistic, with a timeframe for completion. What is your big WHY for a change? In other words, what is your motivation for change? If your goal is not strong enough, change will be short and you will revert to your old habits.
2. Start keeping a gratitude journal. Write 5 things that you are grateful for. Do it either at the end of each day or in the morning before getting out of bed. This will enable you to focus on the positives in your life.
3. Practice meditation every day, and make this your ritual.
4. Get out of your own way. Are you stopping yourself from moving forward out of fear and lack of confidence, or are you afraid of not being good enough? Identify what is stopping you, and act to clear it.
5. Declutter. This includes all the things in your house and the people in your life. Is there a kitchen cupboard that you have been meaning to clear? Is your wardrobe full of unworn clothes? Pay attention to the people in your life, the ones that you spend time with and notice the ones that are toxic, the ones that leave you feeling drained. If they are essential to your life, learn how

to not engage in their negativity. Create a network of people around you who uplift you, who enhance and enrich your life. Decluttering is essential not only to clear the mind, it also creates space for new possibilities to enter your life.

6. Don't give your power away for other to use. It's not their right.

7. Stay away from negativity, and don't engage in other's negativity. Keep a positive mindset and come from a place of solutions, not problems. Negativity keeps people stuck, pushes the blame onto others, and makes excuses.

8. Pay attention to the voice in your head. You know the one: the one that chatters away. What is it saying? Is it telling you that you're not good enough or making you feel guilty? Is it disempowering you? STOP. The stories you tell yourself about you are only true to you. The more you give it your power, the more it will use the power against you. Think about it. Empower yourself with positive language. Use affirmations. For example, "I am good enough." and "I am smart, and I can achieve anything I want."

9. Keep yourself elevated, and keep your vibrations high. This means that you need to connect with your inner self, your core values, and beliefs no matter what anyone says to you.

10. Know your values, personally and professionally. This is key to understanding who you are as a person and what's important to you. Take a blank piece of paper and write 'Personal Values' at the top. Next, start writing values that are personally important to you. Keep writing because there is no wrong or right answer. Now, once you have about 10 to 15 words, choose the value that is the most important to you, and place a [1] next to the word; Repeat for the second most important value and write [2] next to the word; and continue until you have 5. Transfer these top 5 values on a post-it, or write it in your journal. Read them each day. Turn them into affirmations. These values are unique to you.

To find out your professional values, apply the same process with the mindset focusing on what's important to you in your career/job. Again, choose your top 5 from your new list of words.

I f you are ready to stop hiding behind the labels you have given yourself or behind others, and are ready to reclaim your identity to be the best version of you, then Sera Johnston will definitely help you get there.

With over 25 years working in the Training & Development industry, Sera brings a wealth of experience from across the spectrum. She has worked in a top ten FTSE 100 company and as a senior manager in the private sector.

She is a Master NLP (Neuro Linguistic Programming) Practitioner and a Health & Life Coach, in addition to being a published author. Her books are empowering parents across the globe. Her style of coaching is authentic and refreshing because she thrives on empowering her clients from the very first meeting. Sera will be your biggest cheerleader as she knows first hand how important it is to have the right support at the right time - with the right level of accountability.

Sera Johnston
Website: www.serajohnston.com
Facebook: https://www.facebook.com/serajohnston.coaching/
Instagram: @serajohnston
LinkedIn: Sera Johnston

CHOICES: CHOOSING HAPPINESS OVER COMFORT

LINDA GENTILCORE

What do you want in life? A secure corporate job that provides a good, steady income at the end of every pay cycle? With this, for some, comes the daily grind of excessive pressure to perform, an overload of meetings, lean workplaces with unreasonable workload expectations, environments with a low tolerance for mistakes, and constant handballing of issues. Hours upon hours of time at work, occasionally travelling around the country using precious personal time, and trolling the bottomless pit of emails. All for what? A steady income and the corporate lifestyle that comes with it?

'Another day, another dollar!' is what my parents used to tell me when I'd complain about this daily work routine; they were the generation where every dollar was a critical component of survival, with very little left for luxury. My fortunate work life is, however, what I've always known, and this particular work pattern was normal for me, my comfort zone. But really, is being comfortable your dream? **It's not mine.** I've been beavering away, steadily progressing the corporate ladder, and claiming titles in Human Resources (HR) over a 20-year career. It wasn't always as smooth sailing as I had managed to put myself in situations where I'd lost jobs, held jobs that did not align with my strengths or my values, or compromise my family time to meet work commitments.

For the main part though, I truly enjoyed my corporate roles and my life in this world. I enjoyed the perks that came with it— the different social circles, events, and the access to opportunities to learning programs and personal development. I felt virtuous as I was satisfied with the respect others had for what I did and how I operated, which in hindsight is something in itself I took extreme comfort in.

I'm fortunate enough to have an extremely supportive husband who, in my many travel-related absences, did a great job of raising our young family as the dominant parent. He took care of school runs and the majority of the household chores, which resulted in our friends often seeking to clone him. We settled for that stability and comfort on the home front, too.

The first of many realisations truly hit home when I lost my job, and the stability of a corporate job was pulled out from under my feet. During my entire career, I had been exposed to facilitating redundancies, terminating staff employment contracts, and providing solid confidence for many. How is it my own job loss affected me so severely? I realised corporate life had owned me. I was completely reliant on that world. The question beckoned within me: "If HR no longer existed for me, what other work could I do?" I had no other back up plan or alternatives. I was struggling with unfamiliar feelings of loss, fear, insecurity, and uncertainty. I lived in the comfort that the knowledge in the realm of the HR domain would be transferrable and widely sought. I considered the potential of looking for a role in a consulting capacity, but I had not meaningfully maintained networks or contacts with my associates all that well. I was also not truly ready to take the risk.

As I quietly sat by myself in my backyard with no job or readily available options, I asked myself three of the most pivotal questions that shaped my future:

1. What greater purpose or need does my career serve?
2. What new skills have I always wanted to learn?
3. What makes me truly happy?

The answers to these questions did not immediately bubble to the surface of my mind, and they certainly didn't come without shedding a few tears. These tears were for the uncertainty of my future and the intensive bout of embarrassment, shame, and anger that I was suffering. There had been a severe knock to my ego, and there were emotions that I couldn't quite place in my unfamiliar current confused state. With easy access to the tranquillity of the beach, many days during this period were used to obtain peace, to heal and reach out to the universe for answers. Finally, it dawned on me that these big questions were not ready to be answered. A simple focus on one of them was what was needed on my end, and the answer would support me through the future.

I chose to focus on the second question, "What new skill have I always wanted to learn?" I thought about the activities that I enjoyed or that made me curious; this gave birth to a new chapter in my life. I started to learn and discover the art of reading Tarot cards. There was a renewed vision and opportunity brought to life and a possible supplementary career as a Tarot reader. A sense of excitement had been sparked within me!

This whole soul-searching process led to the discovery that my choices directly led to my current circumstances and my career path. I could place no excuses or blame on others! Quite frankly, my choices were not conscious or aware nor did I understand the impacts of my choices. I understood neither my purpose nor what made me happy and it was no wonder that life was simply happening to me. Fortuitously though, I believe everything happens for a reason, so I remained confident that those decisions had their own purpose. I still had hidden underlying doubts.

Choose Why You Do It

Why do we work? Why do we engage in other interests? The answer is fairly straightforward: we want to be happy. So how would *my purpose* contribute to this? Thus, establishing clarity of purpose became an objective. Getting to my life's purpose was not a day's task. It required inner contemplation, and that occurred in many incremental steps.

On reflection, the journey to discerning my purpose started as far back as when I had my first child. Raising a child was my first disquieting exposure to guilt. Being a mother the second time around and resuming my career with two children under 4 made me feel that I was neither performing my corporate role nor my role as a mother well. Converting my mindset was critical to change. I needed to rise from a place of abundance and personal growth, not guilt or resentment over lost opportunities.

Choose to Share

I chose to share my pain with my best friends. It immediately became apparent that we faced similar situations and could support each other to manage various challenges in our work and at home. We set weekly priorities, and we celebrated our wins. This sharing process unknowingly started my initial search for alternative or multi-stream careers based on the premise that in the future I would have flexibility and a greater impact on a larger contingent of people. I became involved in committees, which led to a Board Director opportunity, and through this time launched my first network marketing business. This in itself was something that I vowed never to do! Being part of this support group had the additional benefit of creating closer, and more meaningful, friendships with my best friends, solidifying our friendships forever. Sharing has undeniably been an important ingredient of my happiness journey.

Choose Your Why

My twin sister, also an SCC group member, engaged a mentor. The mentor introduced her to the concept of an 'accountability group', a structured goals group based on '**why**' you want to achieve a goal. Disbanding the SCC method, my sister and I transitioned to the new format with new members as a way of progressing further.

Through the journey as part of the accountability group, I chose to extend my '**why**' to not only feel happy but healthy, confident, and to live with faith. The journey to uncover my purpose continued.

My purpose was greatly influenced by the concepts explained by the international best-selling author Matthew Michalewicz in his book *Life in Half a Second*. He explains that in the context of the time between the world's vast history (documented to exist millions of years before Christ) and that of life which we know will exist well beyond our own current existence equates to <u>half a second in all time</u>. He presents a simple choice to his readers: "How will you choose to use that half a second?" This question assisted me profoundly to rethink my actions and question the purpose of my existence. I wanted to help other people shine and revitalise happiness in life for myself and others.

Both my '*Why*' and '*Purpose*' encompassed happiness for myself and for others. This was, of course, the third and the final question that I had asked myself, back home in my backyard, "What makes me truly happy?"

When I spent the time to journal, I truly appreciated what happiness meant for me. Happiness to me is:

- Growing with my family through love and laughter, sharing every aspect of my life with them, and having faith in their future.
- Having the courage and strength to follow my dreams.
- Having the excitement to live through learning experiences personally and by sharing these experiences with others.
- Connecting deeply with family and friends.
- Contributing and feeling valued in my career and having the satisfaction that these contributions have assisted and enriched people's lives.
- Supporting others positively, laughing, and loving.
- Feeling alive, being active and pain-free, sleeping restfully, and dreaming peacefully.
- Being a part of community groups and causes and making a difference to someone.
- Nurturing myself and enjoying nature's gifts.

Getting to my purpose was not a one-step process, it was achieved through the combination of right tools, the right supporters, and commitment to the process. Happiness is not about choosing to have a career or kids, or both. It's having a life that means something to someone at the end of that life and having lived in the most meaningful way possible. This is my ultimate *why*.

Choose How to Respond

To be truly happy, and not just comfortable with what you have, requires you to master a few key skills. I mentioned that in choosing my **'Why'**. I had to have an abundant mindset. Initially, I couldn't achieve that because when I was between jobs, my mindset was not positive or abundant. If you start with a negative frame of reference or intent, it is going to lead to negative circumstances. The same can be said for a positive frame of reference. Every thought creates a ripple effect, so a positive and abundant mindset is a direct input to likely outcomes. Work in this space takes conscious actions and decisions.

Make Conscious Choices

My colleagues always commented that, "You're always positive." and "You have a fantastic energy when you come in the room." These reactions are a product of how I choose to respond to my environment. Early on in my career, I was exposed to Stephen Covey's *7 Habits of Highly Effective People: Powerful Lessons in Personal Change*. It was the most life-enhancing program, and it truly resonated with me on how I could personally manifest effectiveness and live with more control and choice. I make a conscious choice to be happy at work. I do this despite looming deadlines, pressure, or the type of work that can derail this positivity. I measure the success of my resilience in terms of the forward positive actions and outputs that I can deliver, and I continue to display acts of optimism. Not every response at work or home is aligned to this, but they serve as learnings and reminders to explore the alternatives for improved future choices. They are a part of my tool kit for the future.

Choose How to Live

Living with positivity is also commonly referred to as the Law of Attraction. My understanding of this concept was very limited before reading *The Power* by Rhonda Byrne. The objective of this reading experience is summarised beautifully in the last sentence: *"While you are here, every time you choose the positive, every time you choose to feel good, you are giving your love, and with it, you light up the world."* I now practice giving as much love and gratitude AS is possible each day, and I can attest to the difference it makes and the improvements I feel. My whole sense of being and energy lifts, and I sense that the environment around me is lighter. My day progresses with more flow and satisfaction. Things go right, and I feel great; when they don't, I turn it into a positive and the cycle continues.

Then there is the choice regarding spirituality. There's no right or wrong choice. In my view, it's a choice that one makes in how to live life. I'm a believer. I have faith in life, in life after death, in where I am and where I'm heading, and in the support that exists for me and my family. My spirituality has most commonly been called upon in times of need, support, and direction; I consistently reaffirm its importance in my life by expressing gratitude and appreciation for the choices I make and the experiences I endure. I made my choice, and my life is a product of that faith.

Choose What You Do and Just Do It

The act is to simply set intentions and do it. Theoretically, once I defined my purpose and set my goals and intentions, this should lead to actions. It is, however, only an action if I'm ***actually*** executing it. Often, I find myself gravitating easily to my HR role; it is what I know after all. When I need to act in my coaching, tarot, or health businesses, I find myself having to do so consciously and very deliberately. I acknowledge the existence of procrastination, excuses, or lack of belief. Once acknowledged, then a shift in my mindset is far easier. Action occurs. When I choose to 'do', time escapes me and I'm in the flow.

Through various techniques of life planning, such as goal setting, intention journaling, and vision boarding, I know my aspirations and the steps to get me closer to *my purpose*. These are some of the greatest tools used to help me achieve greater success, vitality, and happiness than I would otherwise have let myself. An intention to act and then executing that intention is a tool that should be used with precise regularity for the largest benefit. Intentions and the use of positive attitude, in my experience, eliminate crippling fear, destructive self-criticalness, and re-affirm beliefs implanted into my subconscious. They make them easier to recall when needed. Clearly, when your attitude aligns with your intention, vitality is truly possible. The act of setting intentions provides a greater ability and acceptance of saying **YES**. *YES* to making choices, *YES* to actually doing, and *YES* to believing in myself.

Yes is influential in the power and energy that it holds; it raises the vibration of positivity and abundance around the environment and creates opportunity. This still needs to be reviewed with good research and smart conscious choices.

Make the Choice

Making the leap from intention to action was tremendously difficult for me while transitioning from being a personal tarot reader to a public reader. Going public meant facing so many demons and being completely uncomfortable. *I was Scared! And worried! And Anxious!* Would I remember what the cards meant? What if the reading had no relevance to them? Would it work for the person? What if they tell people I'm bad? What if I don't know the card and get stuck? The swirl of questions was endless. So, the excuses after the questions also appeared: "I don't have the right space at home." "I don't have the time." "I don't have enough practice." "I'm not good enough."

Choices, choices, choices! How do I respond? Would I do some readings or was I ready to admit defeat and pull out of this potential career stream? I mulled over these questions for weeks, but through the power of *YES*, I set my goal: 'Organise Taste of Tarot invitational day.'

YES! YES! YES! The opportunity had been presented.

In the initial stages, organising the event created a feeling of euphoria, I felt that I was on my way to starting my 'little' business. The date for the tasting session had been set, invites were out, and bookings commenced. I was on a roll. Then the seemingly smooth road got rough. A week before the launch day, my family faced the incoming news of my dad's liver cancer diagnosis. Now, my emotions were upside down, my tarot practice that week was non-existent. The ugly doubtful voices in my head returned, and they resurfaced with all the usual excuses and fears. It was clear, I had to make a choice to cancel or not. It took absolutely all the courage of my conviction to hold on to my *YES* intention and progress towards my goal. I understood the time with tarot and friends would give me reprieve from my dad's situation. So, I made the choice to do it.

YES! YES! YES! The Taste of Tarot day was a huge success! 13 clients along with some awesome confidence boosting readings and others used as learning experiences. Everyone showed up and was so encouraging. It was a perfect start. Since making that choice, there have been many fantastic readings and several soul-satisfying feedback sessions. A client wrote this testimonial after one of my early readings, and it activated a lot of confidence within me. It also **reaffirmed my commitment to my primary purpose of helping others shine**.

"Hi Linda, I've been thinking about our meeting all day today and I want to let you know a few things… I found you thorough, personable and completely accurate! I feel that it's important that you know how good your talent is, numbers are numbers and we can't deny them. Cards are cards and whilst open to interpretation, yours is thorough and concise. Your money each month has been well spent! Your delivery is perfect in the moment of time that you are at, and I shall send others to you. Thank you so much for such a wonderful session, I could have stayed all day had it not been for your motherly duties. I have felt completely inspired all day. Your reading is a complete confirmation of to the journey that I have been denying for many years! Lol – you have lit the torch of my awakening. Thank you so much, it was a pleasure to meet you! You are on the right path!! Xx"

This was so delightful to read. It put tears in my eyes to hear the inspiration that one reading had provided. How truly amazing that one decision to act can lead to so many great opportunities to enhance others and help them grow in their potential and self-awareness.

My purpose was being served in small, yet extremely important doses.

The Moment of Clarity

A further reaffirmed moment of clarity came with the heartfelt loss of my dad within only 5 short months of his initial cancer diagnosis. It was a reality I had never experienced in my life before. The sharpness of hurt and anguish gave me a new purpose: a desire to truly live life to the fullest. I had a renewed conviction to use the power of choice. "Dad would have wanted that" became my mantra.

With Dad's passing, I also had a deeper appreciation of the importance of family. While I loved and cherished my parents, brothers, sisters, nieces and nephews, I became aware that they were being taken for granted in my life. We had quite separate lives, so I made a choice at this time that I would hold the value of my family higher. This was what Dad had worked for all his life. It was his legacy. We continue to heal, but now, we share endless belly laughs, and I have an emotional closeness with my family that is much deeper than in the past.

The conscious choice to be more present with my family is also extended to my children. I chose another change in jobs, one that was closer home. I could do school drop-offs with my daughter most days and reach home in time to share conversations about their days or to nag them to complete their homework. They say they love me, and that is ultimately what counts.

My dad was a bricklayer since he was 11. He worked hard, and it was such back-breaking work. Yet, he was content. Everything was for the family and for day-to-day living. I loved my dad immensely, and he showed me a way of life in which I can be comfortable and content. There is nothing wrong with that. I, however, want experience and deeper happiness above all else. I aspire to share abundance with others, empower people to reach greater potential, and positively impact how they choose to their lives.

I now have a clarity in my life path. I have multiple career options to own and build if I choose. Simple. It's no more difficult than that. Yes. Yes. Yes. There will be challenges ahead, and they'll make me uncomfortable and sometimes stressed, but I recognise that I've made the choice to work towards my purpose and it will continue to serve me greater happiness. Now, I go with the flow and to grow.

Progress is the key.

When developing my teams, I say that if you are comfortable, then you aren't learning; if you're not learning, you're not progressing; and if you're not progressing, then what are you doing? Progress is by far my favourite word. It gives me an assurance that I'm moving forward, and it reinforces that I'm doing what's needed to support my family and to build my vision for the future. I choose to do it. The pressure to **have it all now** has subsided. Happiness, as I have discovered, is in the phase of 'doing and having fun whilst doing it.' Achievements and celebrations are contained in personal growth and happiness, both my own and that of the others who surround me. The destination may signal the end of that, but who wants to reach that point?

Empowered by Choices

Choices will be there forever. Happiness does not come without making the choice to be happy and then executing that intention. Building conscious skills takes practice, so take the challenge and build that skill. These are the choices you have:

- Choose how you respond to that choice.
- Choose the voices you listen to.
- Choose how you will act.
- Choose to believe in yourself.
- Choose decisions that bring you closer to your purpose, irrespective of how insignificant you feel your purpose is.
- Choose what makes you uncomfortable.
- Choose to be present and active.
- Choose to do it.

Be empowered by the choices you have because no one makes the choice for you. Even when you believe that someone else makes the choice, you are making the choice yourself by choosing to act on that. Comfortable is when life happens to you. Life is not connected to a greater purpose or a defined outcome. Comfortable is doing what you've always done, being who you've always been, and thinking and believing what you've always thought or believed. Comfortable is saying things like "It's someone else's fault; I'm always unlucky; Life is just meant to be tough; Nothing ever changes; Nothing's easy; I'm not good at anything and if only…" Take the opportunity to learn from past choices that have led us to a place where things are misaligned, difficult, upsetting, or simply not wanted. These life lessons allow for further choices to directly influence happiness for the future.

Make the choice. That is your power, and that is where true happiness prospers. ***Not making a choice is the only bad choice.***

Linda Gentilcore is a business savvy and goal focussed Human Resources professional. She has used her talents to positively coach hundreds of leaders in her corporate career. She and her husband live in magnificent Australia and have 2 children.

She has a particular interest in diversity with an emphasis on women in leadership. She aims to enhance their career through strengthening their natural abilities. Linda demonstrates an unabiding passion for fuelling her career whilst simultaneously raising her family. In addition, she aspires to help many others shine in their careers and lives.

Linda operates multiple businesses which include businesses based on learned skills in Tarot and Numerology Card Readings, and advocating for good health and wellness. Her 20-year Human Resources career has made her proficient in creating a unique and nourishing experience that is suitable for her leadership and lifestyle coaching.

Linda Gentilcore's inaugural participation in this collaboration is one of many writing projects she has planned. Linda's progresses is noteworthy as she transitions from having a singular Corporate career to being a coach, an inspiring mentor, and an author of the future.

Linda can be reached through her website www.wholesumtransformation.com or www.facebook.com/Wholesum-Transformation-224302938135256/
Photo credit: Photographybysarahd
Linda Gentilcore
Website: https://wholesumtransformation.com/
LinkedIn: www.linkedin.com/in/linda-gentilcore

BE IN A TRANSITIONAL MODE PERMANENTLY AND FIND YOUR INSPIRING JOB

J O A N A   V I S A ,   P H . D .

A re you in control of your life and have room for 'me time'? Can you say that you grow and learn every day? Do you have a strong network? Are you visible? Can you cope with gender-fair situations and lead amazing projects? Do you have an inspiriting job? My answer to all of these is a big yes, and I would like to share my insights with you.

When roughly 94% of Fortune 1000 CEOs are men, what qualities take the rest 6% (who are women) to the most elite levels of corporate leadership? To find out, the Korn Ferry Institute studied 57 women who have been CEOs—38 currently and 19 previously—at Fortune 1000-listed companies and other companies of similar size. Korn Ferry is part of the Rockefeller Foundation's 100 x 25 campaign called the CEO Pipeline Project. It seeks to learn from the women who have already succeeded at becoming CEOs.

Are you ready to jump 'your innovation curve'?

If only 20% of the wealthy people in their 50s are unhappy with their lives, do you want to be one of them?

At School

Reflecting on my childhood in Barcelona, (I was born in 1966) I remember living in a family where being a woman was not really nice. My mother wished for a baby girl, a princess. And after having three boys, I was born. Yes, I was a baby girl, true, but not a princess. I looked like a princess: green eyes, blond hair, and light skin…but nothing more. My family spent every weekend on a farm. There, I loved playing with my brothers outside. We would spend our days looking for small animals, running across the field, and catching tadpoles or small frogs from the water. Dolls never were an option.

My father loved the water as I did. Water meant getting dirty and wet, so wearing my princess badge would have been a bad idea.

My grandma, who celebrated her 102nd birthday a few months ago, loved plants and flowers. She had had a tough time during the Spanish Civil War because her side lost. She could attend a school only up to the age of 7. She has always been my role model because despite having been given few choices in life, she chose very wisely.

During my teenage years, I understood fast that the main rule in our home was simple: if your reports at the school are good, you can do as you wish. I got it. I decided that I will have a very good report and then I will be able to choose and do what I please. It was a nice plan, but what I would learn next is that 'ladies' don't get the same rules. I realised that despite always having better reports than my brothers, I still had to behave like a 'lady.' I still couldn't make the same choices as them. So, I worked and studied harder, it was my only path to freedom.

At the University

In 1984, at the age of 17, it was time for me to decide the course I was going to get my degree in. I was very fortunate to have both a father and a mother with university degrees. I was lucky enough to know that the point was not if I will go to a university or not, but choosing one. I desperately wanted and wished to go to a Drama School. I did not want to be an actress; I wanted to manage actors and become a director. I did not have enough courage to even share this wish with my own mother. I was wrong. This was the first time that I did not raise my hand. I couldn't make my voice heard for the first time.

Well, I thought that if I had to have a university degree, I might as well choose one with a higher acceptance chance. I chose the Veterinarian school. Why? Because in the year that I chose it, there were no Veterinary schools in Barcelona and I would have to move 400 km away. Fantastic. I 'had to' move to another city, meet people, be on my own, and do as I wish.

The decision was made. I would 'have to' go to the North of Spain to attend Veterinarian School. But, alas, it was not to be. The year before I applied, a new veterinarian school was built in Barcelona, only 25 km away from my home. Only 25 km! And not only did I have to stay at home, I even had to share the car every morning with my mum because she was studying at the same campus as me. My goal was to have a higher education so I sucked it up and said: "Yes, mum I will be more than happy to share the car with you every morning." It was my only path to freedom.

First Jump: Biomedical Research

Just after finishing my degree, I was pleased to start working at a veterinary hospital related to my veterinary school. My work was taking care of dogs, cats, and any kind of pets, but it was not enough. My father was a professor at a medical school, and he did his thesis there. So, I did not want to stop my formal education here. I applied to do my PhD in the same veterinarian school I studied. I was working at the hospital with a fellowship, and at the same time, I was doing my thesis (without income).

I was told to work with Leishmaniosis in dogs. Leishmaniosis in dogs is a parasitic illness that can eventually be contagious to humans.

Not a very exciting topic for sure, but my PhD director was one of the cleverest professors, so I said yes.

At last, I had a car of my own! I was so happy to not share it with my mother; as amazing as my mom is, she drives badly. I am amazing, too, and I definitely get my focus and determination from her, but I am a much better driver. So yeah, I was happy to drive myself every day.

The average time needed for doing a thesis is about 5 or 6 years, but my aim was to do in 4. It was 1990, and I was dealing with dogs and leishmaniosis day and night. My working life was great. I learnt and grew every day. I worked hard, and I was enjoying myself.

However, a year later my PhD director called me to his office and asked me out of the blue if I liked dolphins. "The fish?" I asked. He was quick to inform me that dolphins are marine mammals. I was still a bit confused about this line of conversation, so he elaborated: "Because there is an epizootic in the Mediterranean Sea at this moment, thousands of dolphins are dying and our department has been asked to do the diagnostics and find the cause." It turned out that he wanted me to change not only the topic of my thesis but also my PhD director. I said yes. I most probably did not even have another option, but I didn't really care. I wanted to take the risk, so I said that it would be great. After all, all I wanted to earn a PhD, to be challenged, and to explore. This would allow me to do all of those things.

I was lucky. I spent the next 3 years with dead dolphins that had been picked up from the seashore, brought them to the necropsy room, and examined tissue samples. My new PhD director was also clever, so I defended my thesis in 1994.

My first son decided to be born one month before his time, so I defended my thesis just after I gave birth. I had three kids in three years. Even while raising small children, I still was hungry for knowledge, and I needed more. After my second child was born, my contract expired and it was not renewed. I stayed, against my will, without a job for 6 months. What did I do? I enrolled in a university for a six months program related to safety and public health. I did not like it. This was not what I wanted. After these six months, I was hired again. This was the way of life for a young scientist. But I wanted to be there.

I wanted to do more biomedical research. My goal was to climb further in my professional career. I wanted to explore science.

The size of a dolphin is around 1 or 2 metres, and they each weigh 70 to 90 kg. The size of a lab mouse is about 10 cm, and they each weigh about 20 grams. I was offered a chance to move to another department and work with mice instead of dolphins. I said yes because mice were easier to operate on.

During my thesis, my job was to perform the necropsy of the dead animals in order to know what illness they had had. Now, I had to do the same but the small mice. Did you know that mice and dolphins have the same organs: liver, kidney, and even brain? They are all tiny in a mouse, but they are all there.

I carried on my research for ten years. My brain asked for more. My kids were all younger than 5 years. Even so, my family situation was easier to manage because my kids had grown up. I didn't intend to have children right after I got married because I was doing my thesis and I was only 26 after all, but I was so in love with my husband that I said yes. Now I am more than grateful that the father of my kids asked me to do this. Without him, I would not have my three sons now. He is an excellent daddy.

Second Jump: Managerial Role

Next to my office, at the Veterinarian School, there was another door. Have you seen the movie *Monster Inc.*? If you've seen it, there is this place where thousands of doors are waiting to be opened for Sullivan, the huge monster, to open each door and scare the children. I had the same experience: I opened this door, and I met my mentor. She has been there for ten years, and I had only spoken to her about the weather. I knew that if I wanted to take the fast track to the top, I couldn't go there alone.

She asked me if I knew what laboratory animal science was. It is a framework where the animals used for research are protected and studied, and some veterinarians became an animal welfare specialist. Ding, ding, ding, my neurons begun to jump again.

I went to the Netherlands to have a formal education. I was there for only a month, but I came back after learning a lot, and I used it in my work. I attended a programme to become an animal welfare specialist and applied for a new job: to be a veterinarian in charge of an animal facility in a Cancer Institute. I jumped my professional curve again. This was the first time that I had some managerial responsibilities. I had to manage a team and I had to manage the researcher, too. I loved it. First, I got my new credentials; then I got my new job. Learn and jump. Learn and jump.

I began to build my "value model". How can I jump frequently? I had to be in a transitional mode permanently. I wanted to be part of the community of freelance women. I realised that what I need is to follow some basic steps: know myself, challenge myself, connect myself, unleash myself, and then find a job that inspires me.

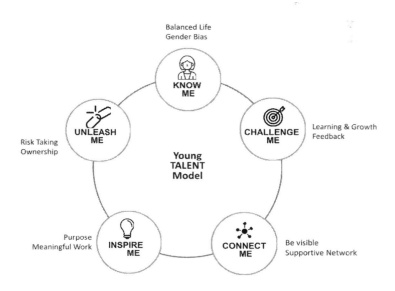

I was married with three kids, had a full-time job, and I fell in love. I fell in love out of the marriage. It was a challenging time for me and my family, and it was time to get divorced. I wanted to be happy; at the same time, I did not want to hurt anyone. The father of my kids had the most generous reaction one could imagine. Even though he did not want to divorce me, we came to an understanding because we had (and still have) strong mutual respect. We still maintain a healthy and friendly relationship now that our sons are adults.

If there are two paths, I always choose the one that I think fits me more, not the easy path. My new partner was a woman. My mother almost collapsed, and my father asked: "Joana, are there not enough nice men in the world?" I had to tell my 85 year-old grandma that I was getting a divorce, and I wished to share my life with a woman. My grandma said: "I'm old, I have done everything in my life. If your husband has hurt you, I am going to kill him with a kitchen knife." Grandma has always been there. I told her that it was never about this.

Around 2002, my kids were all less than 7 years old. I was divorced, had a new job, and was beginning a new relationship with a woman. But I had a new credential: animal welfare specialist. I was determined to use it. Do you know what quality time is? Quality time is the time you spend with someone giving them your full attention because you value the relationship. I applied this concept to my relationship with my sons. I spent, and continue to spend, quality time with my children every day. I do the same thing for all the other people that I care about, too. It works. When I am with my family, no distractions, no mail, no phone calls. I am in. It helps to have a balanced life. There was no space for feeling guilty.

Working as the director of a scientific platform, I realised very soon that I was lacking managerial skills. An animal welfare specialist's job is about animals, not humans. Leadership, human resources management, budgeting, planning, and controlling—these were all my new tasks. My laboratory animal science credentials were not enough, I needed executive tools. So, I decided to get my second masters in Leadership in Science. Needless to say, I learnt a lot.

For more than ten years I was leading animal facilities, but I began to get bored. Was there more? I was invited to take part in a non-profit global organization that promoted the humane treatment of animals in science through voluntary accreditation and assessment programs. I was invited to be a part of the European Council, and I performed animal welfare audits in Europe. I was not alone because I had a mentor to guide me with this new responsibility. He was a clever man. I was very grateful that he mentored me because he believed in me. When I became part of the European Council, I was the youngest member. I was also one of the only two women among the council of ten.

I was using my credentials as an animal welfare specialist and gaining knowledge in management at the same time, but it wasn't a paid job. But who cares? I had my paid job, I loved to travel, I shared time with the other council members, and I liked being an auditor. My grandaunt, who is two years younger than my grandma, said I was a sergeant. Being an auditor seemed to fit me. At this time, I felt the need to move in the direction of quality assessment and legal compliance, so I got my third masters in Master of Quality Management. I had acquired new knowledge; a new door was ready to be opened. So, it continued. I was applying my model again in order to find an inspiriting job: know myself, challenge myself, connect myself, unleash myself, and be inspired. I jumped again.

Third Jump: Executive

When I was around 40, I was offered the position of the Quality Director of my Biomedical Institute. I was going to be a part of the executive committee, where every member excluding me was a man. I remembered my first day at this executive committee, and my voice was not heard. I did raise my hand, and I did share my thoughts. Yet, I did not help my institute move forward. I had failed once again. Never again. I was a woman and I was there.

Every Friday, I would spend some time strategizing. I would ask myself, what's next, Joana? I was not a very good listener at this time; it was difficult for me to keep quiet and listen, even if it is I who was speaking. Therefore, I booked time in the calendar to listen to myself, to know myself, and to know my needs. You cannot have a balanced life if you do not know what your needs and desires are.

In 2014, the general director of my Institute moved on. I had a very good connection with him, so I decided that it was time to look for a new learning—for a new door. My experience with the non-profit association had been so great that I decided to look for a job in that field. I needed an associate executive credential. How? There was a Certified Association Executive program, but it was mainly an American credential. If I got it, I knew that I would be the first one to get it in Europe, and I was.

In 2015, I got my new credentials and then I wanted to find a non-profit entity to manage. The same story again: look for a formal education and jump. I applied for my fourth masters, in Brussels, Belgium—masters for international association executive. The seed was planted and seeded, and I only had to wait for it to flourish. As I've mentioned, if there are two paths, I choose the one that fits me more and not the easy one. I got my animal welfare credential and my association executive credential. I wanted to go abroad and to manage an international non-profit association. It was a good plan.

Fourth Jump: Entrepreneur

My kids were young adults and were still living with me; I was happy with this. In fact, I was more than happy.

It was 2016, and my father had just died. I still miss him. My parents had lived separately for ten years when I was in my second year at the University. Nobody asked me, but I asked to live with my daddy. Neither my mother nor my father wanted me to live with him, but I was determined. I was going to live with my daddy or I was going to live under a bridge with the homeless. My father relented eventually and accepted my decision to live with him. I have a strong bond with my daddy, even now that he is not here.

At work, I was not following the guidelines of my boss, and I did not fit with the new policies. So, I was fired. To be fired is not a disaster, it's an opportunity.

In Brussels, when I was getting my master's degree, I met a German lady who lived there and worked for a non-profit association.

"Do you know what is a coach, Joana?" She said. "Of course, Pep Guardiola from the Barcelona Football club," I answered. She said, "Not really. A coach is a professional who supports people so they can achieve their goals." Subsequently, we built a coaching company together in 2017. I become an entrepreneur when I had crossed 50.

I got married, again, after being in a relationship for more than 15 years. It was an appropriate choice because we wanted to retire in Minorca, a small Mediterranean island.

This is where I am now. At the second launch of our coaching company.

I feel proud of the kind of life that I have built. I jumped the curve several times. I am a freelancer and I am a woman. I have been always in a transitional mode to find my inspiriting job.

I am still applying my own model: I will keep my life balanced, look for new challenges, look for new connections, lead outstanding projects, and find an inspiriting job. If the job that I find is not exciting enough, I will look for new knowledge and begin to look for a new job again. Before I retire, I will jump again. I do not know what I am going to do, but I know how. A new learning is waiting for me. Another door is waiting to be opened by me.

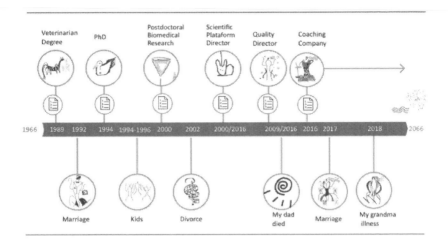

Final Words

I want my story to inspire you and give you tools and tips that you can apply in your own life to take your career to the next level. Here's to you finding your inspiriting job!

As for me, I am always ready to learn, grow, and jump. It has been a great honour to share this with you, and I want to extend my heartfelt thanks go to the compilers of this book.

If you are willing to take your career to the next level, if you want to take the fast track to the top, if you are an executive woman who wants to jump the innovation curve, then Joana Visa, Ph.D. can definitively help you.

She is an internationally certified coach who delights in empowering women so they can become senior executives and impact the world. Joana has accelerated young talented women by guiding them into a new dimension of their selves. Her passion is sharing her own experience as a scientist, as a teacher, and as an executive to launch women into the arena, like the gladiators in Roman Coliseum. She believes that by working with their clients' strengths, every woman can have her 'me time', balanced life, they can grow and learn every day, be visible, lead amazing projects and, finally find an inspiriting job.

You can walk this path alone, spend a huge amount of time, or walk in a partnership with Joana and go faster. If you have a clear purpose in your life, you will be able to see the path. Joana will be there with you. Don't go alone. Go with Joana.

Joana Visa PhD, CAE, ACC
Owner and CEO
35+Executive Women Coaching
Avinguda Alfou, 50 (Sant Julià)
Sant Antoni de Vilamamor 08459, Barcelona Spain
joanavisa@35ewc.com
in/joanavisacoaching/
35executivewomencoaching

3 Hidden Secrets of Transformation

CYNTHIA CAVALLI, PH.D.

Introduction

One day, my life came to a screeching halt. It was a life that I had carefully groomed and curated. It was a life I had trained and studied for. It was something I dreamt of, but it was falling apart before my eyes. I was fond of this life, too. It wasn't absolutely perfect but it had interesting features built in—travel and exploration of ideas—which made it perfectly doable. In all, not too bad for an Indian girl whose grandparents worked in villages and lived in thatched huts. However, fate took an unfavourable turn. Doors that had once been open seemed to close one by one, and I found myself in a place where no one seemed willing to utilise my abilities or even recognize my value anymore. My talents, my educations, and even my hard-won years of experience didn't seem to matter.

Have you ever experienced such crushing defeat in your life? It might have been with your partner, spouse, or even friends. Your personal relationships seem to fray, and your beliefs were called into question. At such times, where do you look for comfort? How can you transform yourself?

Peter Kingsley, an accomplished author who specialises in philosophy, wrote,

> "If you're lucky, at some point in your life you'll come to a complete dead end. Or to put it another way: if you're lucky you'll come to a crossroads and see that the path to the left leads to hell, that the path to the right leads to hell, that the road straight ahead leads to hell and that if you try to turn around you'll end up in complete and utter hell. Every way leads to hell and there's no way out, nothing left for you to do. Nothing can possibly satisfy you anymore. Then, if you're ready, you'll start to discover inside yourself what you always longed for but were never able to find.
>
> And if you're not lucky? If you're not lucky you'll only come to this point when you die. And that won't be a pretty sight because you'll still be wanting what you're no longer able to have…" (Kingsley, 1999, p. 5).

I felt a lot of things during my crisis, but 'lucky' wasn't definitely one of them! And luck aside, I had no idea how to proceed.

In this chapter, I will share three powerful little secrets about the transformation I experienced during my lowest point. These secrets revitalised me, showed a new life, and made me find a new way of being. By following these, I avoided regressing into old habits and patterns.

I said 'little' because they sound simple, but they actually pack a huge punch; and I said 'secret' but that's only because most people in the world seem not to know them. Naturally, they are available for anyone to know; however, the rite of passage of knowing these secrets is hardship and suffering, which any sensible individual would like to avoid. This implies that we're not equipped to deal with troublesome situations precisely because we haven't tackled them earlier. Here is where the power of sharing comes in.

The first secret helps us understand the basic pattern behind all transformation; the second secret reveals the conditions necessary to incubate a new dream life; and the third secret introduces us to a hidden partner who will guide us through difficult challenges into our best possible life.

Before delving into the secrets, I'll contextualise these within my experiences and how they helped me through my troubles.

Sometime in my twenties, I began noticing that my life seemed to shape itself around certain lessons and challenges. These challenges, which often appeared in stages and required months or years to work through, seemed to revolve around certain areas of development. The trouble? I lacked any expertise in these areas. Have you ever felt the same way?

I also observed, much to my dismay, that whatever it was that I most feared—worries over money, breakups with boyfriends, or insecurity about my abilities—inevitably became the focus of the next round of life-shaping lessons. The Swiss psychiatrist Carl Jung noticed this pattern as well and remarked "…find out what a person fears most and that is where he will develop next." (Johnson, 1971, p. 92). Jung also believed that until what is unconscious within us is made conscious, it will direct our lives as fate. This insight offers a key perspective from which we can better understand these disruptive life experiences. It implies that we *can* and also *must* make what is unconscious in us *conscious*. If we do not, it seems our lives will live themselves out anyway but in an accidental, fated way—where we will be lived by our lives and not the other way around.

Jung's model of the psyche can be conceived as a dynamic homeostatic system consisting of three interconnected levels:

1. The first level is the consciousness, or ego consciousness, where we derive our sense of individual identity.

2. The second is the personal unconscious, and it consists of everything we ever once knew or experienced but forgot (also individual to us).
3. The third is the collective unconscious. This is shared across all people and constitutes the ground from which all things arise.

That our psyche is dynamic and homeostatic means that it is self-regulating and seeks wholeness. It is an intelligent living system that communicates with its environment and adjusts its behaviour based on feedback among its constituent parts and environment.

In simplistic terms, wholeness is achieved through a process where what is unconscious *strives* to become conscious, introducing through dreams and waking events experiences that allow us to wrestle with our failings, blind spots, and rough areas in need of polishing. But without a well-bounded ego consciousness, the individual can become overwhelmed. As a homeostatic system, what happens in one part of the psyche affects and can be compensated by other parts of the psyche. Feedback between the conscious and unconscious spheres of the psyche and with the outside environment occurs through dreams and other dynamics that provide information to the dreamer of the psyche's status. One function of dreams, therefore, is to provide feedback about the status of the psyche to the dreamer through images and story.

This whole process occurs not in a linear fashion but in cycles and spirals that deepen with each swirl, moving us through maturing identities over time and bringing us more in line with our authentic identity. So, Kingsley is right. The dead end that brings us to a more genuine version of ourselves is indeed a stroke of luck. Or fate. A normal human life often contains several instances of such major disruption. I've been through it a number of times. Each time, I wasn't sure that I would survive, but when I did, I was gifted with a clearer sense of who I am and who I am not. Of course, I only know all this in retrospect!

I had spent over 30 years developing myself as an aerospace professional. Because it fulfilled my physical and social needs more than adequately, the abrupt end of that phase came as quite a surprise, to put it mildly. My Plan B was to pursue graduate studies in an adjacent field while cultivating long-term relationships in aerospace, which would hopefully translate into consulting opportunities in the future and this ultimately leading to a comfortable retirement. Later, when I was laid off despite my best efforts, I continued forward with the graduate studies, kept my resume updated, and continued to scour the industry for employment opportunities. It was unsurprisingly exhausting. I couldn't see it then, but my professional identity was crumbling. I was no longer who I'd been, but I wasn't yet who I was going to be.

And then came a series of vivid dreams. In each dream, I was trying to return to my old place of work but was thwarted at every turn. Sometimes my desk was given to someone else, or there was no place for me to sit. Sometimes I managed to get into my old building, but no one could see me because I was invisible. Other times, I was invisible and only allowed to work as a janitor. Or I couldn't get anywhere near the building because a bomb was about to explode inside, or a massive fire was raging, or a nuclear weapon carried on a train had just crashed into it. Clearly, I was NOT meant to return to that job/industry/career. I was also suddenly free to do anything I wanted but after following someone else's agenda for so long, I no longer knew what *I* wanted. Although my dreams were crystal clear about what I was NOT supposed to do, they provided little insight beyond this.

As the weeks turned into months and then rolled into years, it became obvious that this particular transition was going to take much longer than I'd initially anticipated. It was an uncomfortable period of profound introspection where I didn't know who I was anymore. Perhaps what bothered me most is that I didn't know how to introduce myself or answer the question "What do *you* do for a living?".

I continued with the process of getting my degree, newly released from corporate obligation and free to research anything at all. And because of the specific and peculiar way my dreams had guided me thus far, I felt drawn to explore the phenomenon of synchronicity, Jung's concept of meaningful coincidence. More specifically, I began exploring the peculiar quality of meaning that was associated with synchronicity, which was referred to by Jung as "objective meaning."

And then synchronistically, as one hoped, the most fortuitous series of events ensued. Teachers, ideas, and helpers began to show up. As it turned out, I realized I didn't *have* to have all the answers, I just had to remain present and available.

It was only when any hope of re-entering my previous profession faded into oblivion, I began to realize that the tide was turning ever so slowly and doors were opening for me once again. I had expected to consult with corporations upon the completion of my degree, but individuals began showing up, wanting to learn how dreams and synchronicity guide us through life. This is how I came to be a coach—by helping clients navigate that dark night of the soul initiation journey.

For this chapter, I have chosen to share the three most powerful secrets that were revealed during my exploration of synchronicity. I encourage you to apply these insights to your own life experiences as you read along because it will surely lead to rich insights and discoveries of your own. When disruptive life events occur, our sense of identity and ideas about the world are deeply challenged. We are forced to *remember* and *reconfigure* our personal identity, our sense of self, and who we are in the world. The proof that these secrets really work lies in the rewards that appear in our outer lives. I trust that these insights will help you as much as they have helped me.

The First Secret

The first secret is really a description of the basic pattern behind all transformation. It is captured in the alchemical saying *solve et coagula*. It basically means 'dissolve and coagulate' or in other words, things fall apart and they come together again in an ongoing, repetetive cycle. This is the fundamental and most basic pattern of all transformation: things must fall apart in order for them to be able to come together again at a higher level or in a completely new form. Of course, what is contained within those two seemingly simple phases is also everything that ever happens. So, this is an incredibly succinct but more importantly a powerful little formula.

This pattern helps us remember that sometimes what feels like death is in reality a clearing of the path for birth to happen. It is not always possible to distinguish between the two, so we must learn to be in a relationship with each of them; we must recognise that they are twin phenomena that partner with each other and maintain the dynamic tension required for life. These phases don't happen only once or sequentially. Life consists of numerous ongoing, revolving, and overlapping cycles of *solve et coagula*, where something is always falling apart to make way for something else, and something new is always coming together.

In corporate life, I found that organizations tend to fear the falling apart phase, so they frequently intervene and do anything to keep things stable. What they don't seem to realise is that by maintaining the status quo, they were in fact keeping new possibilities from materialising. They were actually thwarting the system's natural tendency towards greater maturity and creativity. This, of course, is true in our personal lives, too. People try to maintain life as they know it in its familiar form because the unknown can be frightening.

It is important to remember that not all cycles of transformation are the same. There is one kind that stands out in particular: the initiation. Major stages mark the development of a human being: birth, childhood, adolescence, adulthood, death, and so on. These can, of course, be broken down further, but each of these stages is qualitatively different from each other. A child is notably distinct from an adolescent or an adult, and an adolescent is distinctly different from a mature or elderly adult, most notably in desires and goals. These are obvious transition points that older cultures have always heralded with ritual initiation. Modern life holds far less obvious transition points, such as the loss of a job or career, retirement, and the death of a loved one. Some people find that after doing everything right, everything according to plan, the life that they've been living wasn't really *their* plan at all; it was someone else's—their parents' perhaps, or even society's. Suddenly what had been good enough all along simply won't do any longer. Something deep inside tells them 'No more!', and they are suddenly faced with a conundrum. They must undo everything they've ever known and face the unknown or die inside a little by sustaining a life that is unsatisfying yet familiar.

So, what can we do when facing such a time in our lives? How do we recognise that this is where we are?

How It Might Feel

I can say from my own experience and from the experiences of my clients that the process of falling apart can be very disorienting, but there may be clues along the way that you can pick up before reaching that point. Many times, my clients will tell me that they are sick of themselves or tired of their lives. Their lives no longer feel juicy to them, and they are tired of the stories they tell other people about who they are and what they do. Some people become depressed, and some even feel lost in their own lives. Sometimes, the falling apart is radical and drastic, but the other times it appears more as a general *ennui*, a vague feeling of dissatisfaction that grows unabated. It can also appear as a deep fatigue where tasks that were once easy become exhausting.

Even the coming together stage can be overwhelming because as you change, your perspective and belief systems expand beyond the boundaries of your old worldview. It can be disorienting to discover that the friends and activities you once enjoyed no longer satisfy you. But they didn't change, *you* did.

How It Might Manifest

If there seem to be no outward hints (job loss, death, illness, etc.), our dreams might provide clues that we are experiencing critical aspects of a major cycle of transformation. For example, some people experience apocalyptic dreams, where the world is ending or a home is being destroyed. There may be death dreams, where someone or something is dying (a car, a person, yourself, an animal, or a tree). Some people experience dismemberment dreams, where the dreamer or someone they know is being cut or torn apart. On the other end, people may find themselves pregnant or experience birth. This is not a comprehensive list of the kinds of dreams that may herald this phase in life. So, the best approach is to pay attention, try to capture the essence of feeling in the dream, and record it in an ongoing dream journal.

Some Things You Can Do

Now, let's discuss what you can do about it. I have a couple of simple, yet effective tips that I swear by.

1. Journaling.

This is a wonderful time to begin keeping a journal if you do not already do so.

- Be sure to capture anything that stands out to your mind and heart as peculiar or noteworthy. What moves you deeply? What surprised you? What has disappointed you? What makes you unreasonably happy? This is a good time to become reacquainted with yourself. The chances are that you've changed considerably since the last time you checked in.

2. Keep a copy of the graphic "The Hero's Journey" handy to refer frequently.

It acts as a useful tool that can help you recognize the general stages of personal transformation (especially an initiation) and will do so with a finer granularity than is offered by *solve et coagula*.

- Compare the graphic with your own experience and try to identify where you might be on the journey.
- Make notes of helpers who might appear along the way – animal helpers, spirit guides, dream companions, etc.
- Learn to recognize these characters and develop relationships with them.

The Second Secret

The second secret is something that I call 'the secret womb of creation.' There is a special place for it in the falling apart and coming together cycle that I described in the first secret. It is sometimes described as the *void* or *abyss*, and it often can feel like death but is actually the most essential step that we must undergo in order to successfully realise genuine transformation.

There is a widely prevalent bias in modern culture that anything can be known, and everything must be known eventually. We tend to think of the unknown as a challenge waiting to be solved, but the manifest world is deeper and more complex than we know or even than we *can* know. As finite human beings, our best shot at such mysteries is to engage them by being *in mystery* with them.

In almost every model of transformation, you will find a period (or periods) of uncertainty. In some patterns, it appears as a void, in others as death, and still in others as the period of time following chaos and destruction. It is a time of profound 'not knowing,' and it is essential in gestating the future possibilities that constitute a true transformation.

My favourite illustration for this idea is found in the lifecycle of butterflies. Most people are familiar with the egg, larval, and butterfly stages. The cocoon stage, however, is literally shrouded from view; it is a mystery. What scientists have found is that in the cocoon stage, the larva or caterpillar literally digests itself. Before I describe what happens further, we must back up. While still developing in the egg before hatching, the caterpillar grows what is called an 'imaginal disc' for each body part it will require as an adult (eyes, wings, legs, etc.). Once the caterpillar is born, its job is to eat and to simply stuff itself with leaves as much as possible. As it grows plumper, it also grows longer, occasionally moulting and shedding its skin. Then one day, it stops eating, hangs upside down from a twig, and spins a cocoon around its body (or moults into a shiny chrysalis). Inside the chrysalis, as was already said, the caterpillar or larva digests itself, releasing enzymes that dissolve all tissue except the imaginal discs. These discs can then use the protein-rich, enzyme soup of the caterpillar body as fuel to grow and develop the adult butterfly body parts. If you were to open the chrysalis while the butterfly was developing, you would witness a soupy mess, interrupting the process and killing the potential butterfly.

This is one of the most beautiful and apt metaphors for what happens in the void that I know of. The void is a place where everything we once knew and everything we thought we knew seems to dissolve and disintegrate. Everything familiar has fallen apart, and we find ourselves in a place where we simply do not know anything anymore. Traditional wisdom feels meaningless to us. Even the hard-won tried and true courses of action that brought us whatever success we may have had up till now appear to be worthless.

So, the second secret, the secret womb of creation (or transformation) is…(drum roll please!)… uncertainty. That profound 'not knowing' place. The abyss.

How It Might Feel

What does this place feel/look like in real life? I already described some of how it feels, where tried and true wisdom seems to hold no insights of any use. That quote by Peter Kingsley at the beginning of this chapter also describes the feeling of finding yourself at an absolute dead end, just knowing that no matter which way you turn, it will be the wrong way.

Jungian analyst Marie-Louise von Franz calls it a paradox.

"People come to the consulting room," she says, "and lay out a collision of values with great embarrassment and agony. They want resolution but they would have something even greater if they could ask for the consciousness to bear the paradox…It is precisely here that one will grow. Paradox is brought to its next stage of development by a highly conscious waiting. The ego can do no more; it must wait for that which is greater than itself." (von Franz, 1970, p. 4).

In other words, the dead-end intractability of this place is actually a feature, not a bug. It is *meant* to be a situation without the solution.

Turning to von Franz's insightful words, "the unconscious wants the hopeless conflict in order to put ego-consciousness up against the wall, so that the man has to realize that whatever he does is wrong, whichever way he decides will be wrong.

This is meant to knock out the superiority of the ego, which always acts from the illusion that it has the responsibility of decision…To consent to paradox is to consent to suffering that which is greater than the ego. The religious experience lies exactly at that point of insolubility where we feel we can proceed no further. This is an invitation to that which is greater than one's self." (von Franz, 1970, p. 4)

You are not supposed to know what is going to happen or what can happen. You are meant to not know because in that place of supreme not knowing the 'powers that be' are fashioning from *your* imaginal discs the new you that you will next become.

How It Might Manifest

Dreams that indicate our presence in this stage sometimes include imagery of inundations— being flooded, being overrun with water, or even a deluge. Sometimes people find themselves at a crossroads or stuck in a car or boat with no way out. I've had dreams of being in a frozen wasteland, lost in the desert, or the ocean. Again, these are examples of what such imagery *might* indicate.

Here is a synthesis of how various clients have described their experience in this place:

"I'm in that 'not knowing' place again! But it's ok because I know eventually, I will get a sign … like an arrow pointing to the next step. And eventually I'll get another sign and take another step, and another, till finally I will find myself in a different place, in a new life."

Some Things You Can Do

Since being stuck is really the whole idea of being in this place, now is not the time for action. At least not the kind of action that we're used to taking, where we rally forces, make plans and rush forward. Waiting plays a huge role in what happens here. It can be a supremely uncomfortable time because our action-loving culture doesn't make allowances for people who *wait*. This is a time to *incubate*, which contrary to appearances is an active process, where the action takes place below the surface.

One of the most challenging aspects of the void, for me, is what to tell others I was doing during this time. It is helpful to come up with answers ahead of time to allay the curiosity of others while vouchsafing your private process. You can tell people you are pulling together a special project, whose concept is still in development. You can say you are working on a book, play, or story. Because more than anything, this is *not* the time for outside scrutiny into your inner processes (excluding the therapeutic relationship of course). Remember, cutting open the chrysalis kills the butterfly. It's not even the time for *you* to scrutinize your inner processes, let alone someone else.

The void holds many gifts, and there are ways of feeding the processes that create the new you. This is a good time to take up creative projects, such as painting, gardening, cooking, or creating and playing music. Try to find activities that utilise the parts of your brain that, to this point, have been underutilised.

Here are some of things that I recommend.

1. Engage your "inferior" function.

Now is a good time to gently focus on your weak areas of development, known in Jungian psychology as your *inferior function*.

What does this mean? Well, if you are an engineer, you might be a thinking type, for example. So, *feeling* activities such as creating artwork would be a good activity for when you find yourself in the void. If you are an artist who normally flies by the seat of your pants, you might consider lending your services to a community project that needs help with oversight, planning, or organizing. If you are a feeling type, you might focus on the details of a news story or legal argument and tease out the pros and cons, positive and negative elements of the various arguments to construct a sound summary— in other words, exercise your *thinking* function.

Now, the goal isn't to become your opposite type, but to simply *exercise* activity in our weak areas as it rejuvenates our personality, which may have become tired from overuse in its normal mode.

2. Focus on what the heart desires.

Modern society tends to be overly action-oriented and achievement-focused. Now is the time to do what the heart loves to do. Some people may need a reminder of where their heart even is! If you normally focus on others, take some time to focus on yourself; do something nice for yourself that you might not otherwise do, like taking yourself out on a special date.

If you normally focus on yourself, now is a great time to do something nice for someone else, for no other reason than that it would make them happy. It could be a friend who is not expecting it or even a stranger.

3. Pay attention to the symbolism in your dreams; notice synchronicities and unusual occurrences.

That journal you created for the previous secret will really come in handy now. Once you start collecting your dreams, synchronicities, and other odd incidents, you should be able to notice patterns within the events threading through your life. Those patterns may provide clues to the ultimate direction of your new path.

4. Divination

You can try this activity to help you see the bigger picture regarding what is happening in your life. It won't give you answers to specific questions necessarily, but it may help alleviate some of the anxiety that you may be experiencing by not being allowed to take action or know what is coming. You can use tarot decks, angel cards, a pendulum, or even tea leaves.

Whatever you use, try to pose your questions with a grateful heart, trusting that the universe, or God, or your higher powers have insight and perspective that you do not in this limited, embodied form. And that what is happening is probably exactly what you would choose if you could see everything the way they do.

The Third Secret

The third secret is a little harder to put into words. It concerns an aspect of nature that pervades reality but because of the predominant bias in modern culture towards a scientific, causal perspective, it remains largely hidden. Modern culture tends to believe that everything that exists came about because of something that happened previously. But causal relationships are only one of the ways that the world we observe and experience comes into being.

Another way is through meaning and meaningful events but not in the way that we normally think of *meaning* as a human-constructed, rational thought process. Jung saw hundreds (if not thousands) of individuals in the course of his psychology practice. He had already formulated his ideas of the personal unconscious, which had similarities with Freud's ideas, when he began noticing unconscious structures in the human psyche that shared similarities across individuals and even cultures and civilizations, giving rise to his idea of a *collective* unconscious—one that is shared by all of us but which may manifest differently within each of us depending on the age and culture in which we are born. He also noticed that what occurred in the dreams of his patients often mirrored what occurred in their waking lives, as if consciousness and the unconscious were engaged in an ongoing and dynamic dialogue. This process, which he termed *individuation*, seemed to be directed towards a goal: the development of the individual towards *wholeness*.

I mentioned the concept of synchronicity earlier, also known as meaningful coincidence. Jung proposed that in addition to events unfolding as a result of causal influences, they also appear to occur through synchronicities or meaningful coincidences. These are *not causal* at all. In fact, he stipulated that there could be no way that the two synchronistic events could possibly be related causally.

An example of this was shared by a Jungian therapist whom I know. He had a patient coming in for marital counselling, who simply could not seem to recognise the magnitude of his problems. In exasperation, one day the therapist threw up his hands exclaiming "Your marriage is like a car wreck!" Just at that moment, there was a loud car crash right outside the office window. The uncanny juxtaposition of the therapist's words 'car wreck' and the explosive car wreck occurring outside shook both of them to their core.

Note that the car accident did not *cause* the therapist to say those words nor did his saying those words *cause* the car accident. This was an acausal coincidence, but it still was one that was highly meaningful for the therapist and his patient. Not every coincidence is equally meaningful or momentous (or even simultaneous). Some are silly, incidental, and even nonsensical, but the others carry great weight. It is worth paying attention to this last category because its exploration can yield some very helpful insights.

I've also already mentioned that once my old life fell apart, and I finally stopped trying to find my way back to it, a new world seemed to open before me. It could also be that I had simply found my way to a new way of seeing and what had been there all along was revealed. The world is more connected at a deeper level than I'd ever understood before. *Meaning*, it turns out, is a profound connecting factor in the universe. It is not the kind of meaning where we puzzle out what is happening or think things through rationally and not necessarily in the stereotypically 'new-age' way where 'the universe wants you to have everything you desire' (a misunderstanding of the Law of Attraction). Instead, it is a deeply mysterious way which I am still learning and will continue to learn. As a result of this search, my beliefs about fate and destiny have changed. I now understand them as distinct, intelligent, and dynamic factors that influence and direct the events in our lives. In fact, in story after story, it almost seemed as if the future *knew* what it wanted from an individual and bending backwards through time, it shaped events towards its desired goal.

This is impossible to see when you are right smack in the flow of events, but it becomes more obvious looking backwards.

How It Might Feel

But even this does not present the entire picture of the secret. Because of my scientific training, I believed that the universe was not personal, and the things that happen to us are random. I even believed that our existence is random. My research findings on personal experiences of synchronicity directly contradicted this belief. Not only is our existence not random, it appears that we are *meant* to be here. This factor of meaning that Jung described as 'objective' (to differentiate it from the more familiar 'subjective' and personally constructed form of meaning) became personified for me as a helper and guide, along with Fate and Destiny.

So, this is the crux of the third secret: there is a connecting principle hidden in the realm of nature that is dynamic and alive, and it is possible to relate to it in personified form, as a real person. For me, this form of meaning appeared as a goddess—a goddess of meaning. For Jung, it appeared as a god of meaning. I became aware of her presence very slowly and gradually, only when I was very still and not trying to be anywhere or accomplish anything. Jung likened her to the Tao in the *Tao Te Ching*.

> Here is an excerpt that describes her:
> There is something formless yet complete
> That existed before heaven and earth.
> How still! How empty!
> Dependent on nothing, unchanging,
> All pervading, unfailing.
> One may think of it as the mother of all things
> under heaven.
> I do not know its name,
> But I call it "Meaning."
> If I had to give it a name,
> I should call it "The Great."

(From the Tao The Ching by Lao-tzu, Ch. XXV, as quoted in Jung and Pauli's The Interpretation of Nature and the Psyche, p. 97, 1955).

I cannot begin to express in words how she has changed my life. I even dreamt that I was giving birth to her. She informs my life with a depth of meaning that I'd never imagined possible. Whether or not you experience this dimension of meaning in personified form, there are certain characteristics of synchronistic, or objective, meaning that are important to remember.

There is a distinct difference in the kind of meaning and understanding that arises from conscious attempts to puzzle out the meaning of an event and when we are suddenly and instantaneously *hit* by the meaning of an event. The latter is closer to the kind of meaning that is found in synchronicity. Of course, meaning that has been puzzled out and rationally derived is also valuable, but this isn't an either-or situation. Both are valuable, and both are necessary. They are, however, vastly different animals.

People who've experienced what Jung termed 'objective meaning' describe it as a lightning download experience—they knew instantly something or everything about a situation. They just *knew*. One woman described receiving a whole PowerPoint presentation for an important client this way. Another woman described how a chain of very painful and devastating losses suddenly resolved themselves fully with the birth of her niece, which coincided synchronistically to some special dates and numbers. Another man described it saying: "Something in you knows your fate, and the way that you are supposed to go, and if you go a little off track, you may get a dream to show you the way to get back on track!"

Notice that it is also not quite the same phenomenon that is addressed by the Law of Attraction. The Law of Attraction basically means that we attract whatever we focus our attention on, and we can create intentions that manifest in our reality. This is a distinct feature of reality better captured by the medieval doctrine of 'the sympathy of all things,' which seems to govern both the Law of Attraction and synchronicity.

But synchronicities occur outside causality and intention. They tend to occur more frequently during periods of great stress and change, as might be expected during deep transformation. They appear to be complex in nature, and this is the subject of some exciting research being conducted by several scientists and analysts. But for our purposes, it is helpful to recognise that they are different and that meaning in synchronicity is not constructed but revealed.

How It Might Manifest

The focus of this chapter is on certain hidden secrets that can help us navigate disruptive transformations. Synchronicities and synchronistic dreams are the hallmarks of major life transformations. This means that you may notice your dream life is suddenly very active and vivid and may even contain precognitive information or foreknowledge of things to come. You may find that the information that comes to you in your dreams also breaks into your waking life in strange ways. In one incredibly painfully destructive but educational year, nearly every dream that I recorded in my journal came true—maybe not in the way that I would have imagined, but true nevertheless. I dreamt about my future husband, future home, future daughter, and future work assignments. That was a very significant year for me in terms of life transformation. And, it's not as if I could actually do anything about the information from the precognitive dreams. I couldn't buy a lottery ticket and win big, for example, but it did give me a profound feeling of being connected to this world and this reality. It made me feel like I mattered, even if I wasn't quite sure how. When a synchronicity happens to you, especially when it is profound, it feels as if God from heaven reached down to tell the little-insignificant-you a secret. It feels as if life *knows* something about you that it can't possibly know. It feels as if your existence on this planet is not an accident.

What it does *not* do is give you an inflated sense of self or importance. Instead you realise that everything that exists has its own part to play and its own place in the larger scheme of things. You realize that your own personal role is important, recognized, and valued. Somehow receiving that glimpse of the larger picture within which our small lives occur is incredibly healing. Just the fact that our smaller life has its rightful place in the larger scheme of life is healing.

Some Things You Can Do

I've already mentioned the importance of keeping a dream journal. It not only captures what has happened but makes it possible for you to discern direction and trajectory of your dream stories. I can look back at my old dream journal and recognise the themes that emerge in various dream, and see exactly how I was being led in my development. Sometimes, it is even possible to detect the direction of my life, which can provide enormous relief, especially if you happen to find yourself in the abyss. It can be very helpful, and even healing, to recognize all the paths that life has led you through without letting you down.

You can also include any of the exercises shared in the other secrets. They are helpful, no matter where you are in your personal process.

Another helpful exercise is active imagination. This is an exercise where you can begin a dialogue with any characters who appear to you from dreams or non-ordinary states of attention, as might occur during meditation, reverie, or shamanic drumming. As you get more proficient with your active imagination, you may find your experience of the world becoming more dynamically alive. You may naturally begin connecting spontaneously with non-humans in your life, like your pets, the wild animals you encounter, the sun, the moon, the grass, and the air! It is a wonderful and rejuvenating way to live.

Final Words

One day, the golden life I worked so hard to create fell apart, and I agonised over why I didn't feel more fulfilled and why my career seemed to fail while those of my colleagues succeeded. But what I learned during these painful years is that sometimes life *does* know who we are, even if we ourselves have forgotten. Life, which brings all things into being and lets them go when their time is done, absolutely does bring us into this world at a specific time and place to accomplish what only we can do. It is a big gamble because there's no assurance that we will be successful, but life seems willing to take the chance. It's up to us to show up, to remember who we are in the very depths of our souls, no matter what adversity befalls us, and to play this game all the way with honour and integrity.

If you find that your life is falling apart, it may be because it is time to transform into a new way of being in the world. It may feel daunting but as the comparative mythologist Joseph Campbell said about the hero's journey (which is what this particular initiating transformation is really about):

> "We have not even to risk the adventure alone, for the heroes of all time have gone before us—the labyrinth is thoroughly known. We have only to follow the thread of the hero path, and where we had thought to find an abomination, we shall find a god; where we had thought to slay another, we shall slay ourselves; where we had thought to travel outward, we shall come to the center of our own existence. And where we had thought to be alone, we shall be with all the world." (Campbell, 1968, p.18)

And finally, in closing, I'll share a favourite quote by the Austrian poet Rainier Maria Rilke from his *Letters to a Young Poet*. I encourage you to keep both of these quotes close in your heart as you navigate the difficult straits of a major transformation.

> "So you mustn't be frightened ... if a sadness rises in front of you, larger than any you have ever seen; if an anxiety - like light and cloud-shadows, moves over your hands and everything you do. You must realize that something is happening to you, that life has not forgotten you, that it holds you in the palm of its hand and will not let you fall." (Rilke, 2011, p. 38).

Life breaks us open, again and again; each time it releases precious gems, golden nuggets of insight, polished through our struggles and triumphs, until they shine with unimaginable splendour. This is the goal of life: to disrupt and transform in the service of consciousness. May you find your way to your best life ever!

Cynthia Cavalli is many things: a shamanic dream and synchronicity coach, corporate systems futurist, complexity consultant, and visionary life strategist. Her background is an eclectic blend of education and experience, including a doctorate in human systems/organizational psychology, three decades as an aerospace engineer, an MBA with coursework at Cambridge University, and certification as a Shamanic dream teacher. She hails from South India and enjoys incorporating insight and expertise from diverse cultures around the world. She is equally at home doing a lot of things: providing leadership coaching to corporate executives and systems, providing complexity workshops for groups, and guiding individuals through the life's uncertain passages using dreams, synchronicity, stories, and mythology. She is a gentle, wise soul dedicated to global transformation through personal inner work, and a marriage of objective science and intuitive healing practices.

To contact Cynthia Cavalli, Ph.D.:
Website: www.cynthiacavalli.coach
Facebook: https://www.facebook.com/CynthiaCavalliCoaching/
Instagram: https://www.instagram.com/cynthiacavallicoaching/
LinkedIn: https://www.linkedin.com/in/cynthia-cavalli-ph-d-8620ab2/

A Blessing in Disguise

DARREN HARRIS

"Every positive thing in your life represents a single unique blessing. Every negative thing in your life has the opportunity to become a double blessing. For when you turn a negative into a positive, you gain twice. You are no longer burdened with the negative situation, and in addition to that you are strengthened by a new positive force."

Ralph Marston

This passage is more than a quote, it is a way of living. No matter who you are, you will experience a stressful life event that changes you in some way. But what I hope to show you is that we can transform these challenging situations into something we can treasure. We don't achieve success despite these challenges, but because of them.

The Pleasure of Pain

When I was fifteen months old, I was diagnosed with bilateral retinoblastoma, a form of childhood cancer that resulted in my right eye being removed and my left eye being treated with radiotherapy. The radiation destroyed any cancerous cells in my eye; however, it also caused permanent, irreparable damage to some of the healthy tissue in and around my remaining eye. Over time, my eyesight began to deteriorate, as did the eye itself. It became scarred and discoloured due to a lack of moisture owing to the fact that I could not blink or close my eye.

One day, I was visiting my aunt's house and my cousin there as well. I was perhaps seven years old, and she was 4.

You've probably noticed that children say or do things without thinking, which can result in embarrassing and even hurtful situations or actions. Even adults are prone to acting impulsively occasionally but thankfully we get better at controlling our impulses as we grow older.

When my cousin saw my eye, the reaction was like a scene from *Doctor Who*. She ran and hid behind the sofa, crying hysterically and refusing to come out. The adults reacted as anyone would. They went to comfort her, but not one of them thought to come and help me. No sobs were heard and no tears were seen, but I was hurting too. My suffering just happened to be silent.

I tried almost everything you can imagine to hide my eye: looking away from people, wearing sunglasses, cosmetic shells, and refusing to use a cane. I even considered getting it surgically removed and having a second glass eye fitted. After all, prosthetics were so good by that time that most people couldn't even tell that they were fake. But who was to be the beneficiary of all this hiding? Was the whole purpose of doing these things not to frighten little kids? Was that enough of a reason to do this? Some part of me felt defiant. None of these things made me feel any better. If anything, they were making me feel worse. I was just papering over the cracks.

It seemed to me that avoiding pain and seeking pleasure is a big part of the human motivation. Pain is associated with illness and injury. At an early age, I discovered that pain couldn't be avoided. And as I grew older, I came to realise that it <u>shouldn't</u> be avoided either.

What motivates you? Do you want more pleasure in your life? How much pain are you prepared to go through to get what you want?

Beware of the pleasure trap. Pain and pleasure are not opposite ends of the spectrum. Pain comes first. When you prepare for pain, you experience guilt-free pleasure. This isn't a green light for anyone to self-harm, but there is recognition that in everyday experiences, you are going to have to go through varying degrees of discomfort to get what you really want.

Means to an End

Less widely used than it once was, the eleven-plus exam determined children's admission into selective secondary schools. People who believed intelligence was genetic and therefore fixed saw streaming as a good move. Streaming split pupils based on their academic ability, and it was a widespread practice. It put pupils in a clear top-to-bottom hierarchy, based on their perceived ability to follow different curricula.

I passed the eleven-plus exam with flying colours. In other words, I was officially one of the brainy kids. But I wasn't the only one. I started off performing well, but as the pecking order established itself, my work started to deteriorate. Before long, I was getting Ds and Es. The problem... well, there were many. I turned up to lessons late, I forgot to bring my books, I messed around in class, and I didn't hand in my homework. The logical solution was for me to just do the opposite to what I was doing. That would have fixed it, but I didn't feel like it.

After one particularly poor performance, my maths teacher, in exasperation or perhaps desperation, exclaimed "Darren, you can do better." Sadly, I didn't hear her words for the critical encouragement that they were. What I heard instead was my inner voice saying "Better than whom? Definitely not better than Jack, he's the whiz-kid who can remember the first 100 digits of pi. Surely not Andrew either, he's the swat who revises for 12 hours straight." No, I definitely wasn't anywhere near their league, so how was I supposed to do better than them? What my teacher meant was that I could improve my own performance irrespective of anyone else's. "You can do better" was such a simple statement but an irrefutable truth. My work was worse than it was before—that was plain to see. The word better is a comparative, true, but my teacher and I, we were comparing different things. She was comparing my current performance to my past work, and I was comparing myself to other pupils. I was the one setting an unfair standard, not her.

When the penny finally dropped, I focussed on my own performance instead of that of others and I started moving up the league table. My grades improved—first Cs, then Bs, and eventually As. I had achieved what I wanted all along but although it was the same end, it was by different means.

Comparing people against one another is as old as humanity itself, but it reached a whole new level just before the First World War. Psychometrics, the measurement of psychological characteristics in relation to the whole population, became the norm, in which the utopian dream of greatly improved productivity could be achieved by fitting every man, woman, and child to the kind of work each was most suited to.

Who do you find yourself being compared to? Who is making the comparison? What effect is it having on your sense of well-being? Does it make you feel envious or discontent?

Beware of the comparison trap. Feeling good or bad about yourself based on whether you are 'better' or 'worse' than another person isn't a sustainable model for happiness. Someone once said that "comparing yourself with others makes you bitter, comparing yourself with yourself makes you better." After all, some days your competitor is just going to do better than you, and the only crumb of comfort you'll have is knowing that you did your best.

The Success of Failure

Going to university was more of an obligation than an option that happened because I had reached the required academic standard. The standard had successfully harnessed an environment in which enrolling at a higher education institution was the natural order of things. My schooling could socially be considered a success.

However, the first thing I learned while at university was how to drink. After all, almost everyone I knew drank alcohol. Fresher's week became fresher's month, and fresher's month became fresher's year. While some went to the University of Life, I had a life at university.

I scraped through to my final year but then came the milk round: that time of year when large organisations visit careers fairs to promote their graduate training schemes. I was suddenly contemplating life after university. An upper, second-class degree was the golden gateway to dream jobs. The best employers recruited only the best graduates, and I wasn't anywhere near the best.

Even though I wasn't studious by any measure, getting my work done typically involved a laborious six-step process. I had to go to lectures, borrow a fellow student's notes afterwards, get someone to read them to me (who was capable of deciphering handwriting that wasn't their own), make my own notes using a Braille machine, complete whatever assignment I had been given, and then read it aloud to a scribe who would put my work to paper, using all the intricacies of the Greek alphabet, integral signs, superscripts and calculation layouts that are important in the world of mathematics.

I graduated with lower second-class honours, which was (un) affectionately known as a Desmond. I was bitterly disappointed, not because my degree classification had ruled me out of so many career opportunities, but because it was a source of shame. After all, those who got a 2:2 were labelled either too lazy or too stupid for the university in the first place.

But there were kids I knew who got top marks all the way through and yet failed to get a job straight after graduating. I learnt a lesson no textbook could ever teach: Over time, the value of a qualification decreased as one's experience increased. Although you think your world depends on a piece of paper containing a few distinguished letters, there are always bigger tests ahead.

Do you have a fear of failure? Does it stop you from doing the things you need to do to achieve your goals? Do you consider your life to have been a success?

Define success on your own terms. Judge failure by your own rules. The reality is that only you can ever know your struggle, and explaining it probably comes across as sour grapes. So, be proud of your achievements, no matter how hard people try to take them away.

Centre Stage

In the summer of 1996, I travelled to Atlanta Georgia for the Paralympic Games. With the weight of disposable income in my pocket, I was there for a holiday of a lifetime.

Atlanta was the birthplace of Martin Luther King Jr., a renowned civil rights leader who inspired a generation of activists like no other. At his museum, I heard a replay of his greatest speech, and such was its impact that I was transported in time. I felt as if I was one of the 250,000 civil rights supporters gathered around Lincoln Memorial on 28 August, 1963.

But as I was walking through the gates of the Centennial Olympic Stadium several hours later to watch the closing ceremony, I was eminently aware that I didn't have a dream of my own. On centre stage were athletes from every corner of the globe, some of whom had made their dreams come true. It was a brilliant spectacle, but I was a mere spectator.

Yet, mysteriously, when I heard the crowd chanting the names of their heroes in unison, I had an epiphany. All of a sudden, it was as if I could hear my own name and my dream was born. I knew in that instant I wanted to be a Paralympian. At that time, I had no idea it would take me the next twelve years to join the club. At school, sports had been my saviour, giving me a way to vent unresolved anger and frustration. But it was more than that. Sports was my passion, something woven into my DNA. There is something powerful about being in a crowd. It lets you blend in, hide, and even find anonymity. It gives you something to belong to. There is safety in numbers and in knowing you can go with the flow.

But how can you make a massive difference in the direction of your life whilst sitting in your armchair? How can you make your dreams come true if you don't have a dream? Give up your seat. Don't spend your life waiting on the sidelines watching others succeed. Step out and play the starring role in your own drama.

Making Kings from Pawns

In the summer of 2004, blind football made its inaugural appearance at the Paralympic Games in Athens. We qualified for a place in the competition by the virtue of getting to the final of the European Championships in the previous year. However, disaster struck a few months before we were due to fly out to Athens. With the exception of England, the other three home nation football associations would not sanction us to compete as Great Britain. As the captain, I had written to the Scottish, Welsh and Northern Irish chief executive officers, begging them to overturn their decision but my plea fell on deaf ears. The dream was turning into a nightmare, and eight years of blood, sweat, and tears were in danger of being washed down the drain.

One strategy was playing a waiting game and see if the football associations would reverse their decision come the next Paralympic Games in 4 years' time. (As it panned out, that is exactly what they did. However, at the time that I was weighing up all my options, there were no guarantees that would happen.) An alternative strategy was pursuing a completely different line of attack and making my recreation my vocation.

Life is like a game of chess, the kings live in their palaces and manoeuvre the pieces around the board for their own purposes, sacrificing pawns when and where they see fit. Every move you make can either bring you an advantage or a disadvantage. Your best-laid plans can be left in ruins, and ill-thought-out decisions will teach you to think twice the next time. But until the king is trapped, the game is still on.

Do you regret your past decisions? How do you know if things would have turned out better had you chosen a different course of action? Do you anticipate things going wrong even before you've given it a try? Do something different. There's an old saying that if you always do what you've always done, then you will always get what you always got.

When you approach a problem from another direction, you encounter a new landscape, one with different problems you may be better equipped to solve. Give it a go. It may just change your life.

The Opposite of Obvious

The monumental move I made was to quit my IT job and make a career out of my hobby, judo. Of course, the numbers didn't add up. I was giving up a good salary, a company pension, and a generous holiday entitlement. There was even the possibility of a promotion on the horizon. But it wasn't just the 100-mile-a-day commute that tipped the scales, it just didn't feel right. In the six years leading up to that point, I had spent all my workdays housed in an open plan office, sitting at a Formica laminated desk, and surrounded by artificial plants perched on top of steel grey cabinets.

It dawned on me one day that I wasn't living by the company values that were embossed in a large font on meeting room doors. 'Freedom' and 'fun' were two of the values that I truly desired, but writing code wasn't fun and I really was a slave to the wage. As if in a state of learned helplessness, I was in a prison of my own making. Perhaps by design, the company was going through its own transition and was offering a voluntary redundancy programme. The signs were all there, and they were pointing in one direction. The ticket to freedom was on the table. Only one thing stood in my way: once I put my name forward, there was no turning back. I couldn't think of many irreversible decisions I had made up to that point in my life, but this one was going to be huge. After all, I had to pay my mortgage and household bills, fill the fridge (athletes eat a lot of food!), and get to and from training— with no guaranteed income to fund any of it.

When my notice was accepted, the news spread like wildfire and I became the subject of office gossip. "Which company are you leaving for?" was the most frequent question. The first assumption made was that I was going to one of our competitors in the industry. "How much extra are they paying you?" was next in line. The assumption was that the offer of more money had lured me away. Of course, both assumptions were wrong in my case. I had no intention of doing the same job in a different place. I was simply following my dream and unfathomably, I wouldn't receive a penny for it in the short term.

My replies drew gasps of amazement, if not outright derision. They just couldn't believe that anyone would do something so ridiculous. Outside of work, the responses were similar. Even my own mother, who had supported me through thick and thin, thought I had lost the plot. The negative feedback loop surrounding my departure heightened my sense of doubt. I was flying in the face of history and logic, but it also strengthened my resolve.

There are always options open to you in life, whether you realise it or not. You can do the obvious and stay on the well-trodden path millions have travelled before you, or you can do the opposite and go against the tide of popular opinion. The latter will let you do things that are yet to be discovered. Leaving is never easy, but I was certain that staying in a job I was unhappy in would have led to worse consequences.

Have you ever been on a great holiday? What made it great? Was it the thought of escaping your bleak surroundings, or something pleasant over the horizon? How did you feel about going back? Were you filled with dread? Go your own way. There is always a point of no return. Sometimes, you have to get a one-way ticket. But when there's no turning back, you begin that journey with 100% commitment, and that's exactly what you will need to get you through the tough times.

The Novice Master

I had already earned the coveted black belt by the time I began my full-time judo training. In martial arts, a black belt usually denotes that the wearer can demonstrate the basic techniques of the discipline with a high degree of competence. In judo, it meant that the examiner awarded scores for no less than 67 throws, 12 holds, 13 arm-locks and 11 strangles. A black belt is a sure indicator that you are no longer considered a novice, but it doesn't make you a master either.

The next four years weren't about mastering everything; at the elite level, the top performers specialise in a handful of techniques. A highly refined skill lets you perform a technique in a game setting. That can take thousands of hours of practice under the watchful eye of a coach. You practice the smallest nuances of a technique over and over again. You have to know the technique inside out—everything from how you modify it for particular opponents to how they might defend against it or even counter it until it becomes second nature.

The arduous work paid off. I did qualify the final place at the 2008 Beijing Paralympic Games as the lowest ranked player on the list. Unbelievably, in the first round of the competition, I was drawn against the reigning world champion from Cuba. It was an examination like no other; four years of hard work thrown away in less than a minute and no retake for another four more years. My hopes of a Paralympic medal dashed, I was down for days. But when the gloom lifted, I came to see the qualification itself as my greatest ever achievement. Judo was a sport that I had participated in for less than a decade and there I was, against all odds, competing with the best in the world.

For me, the Paralympian embodies equality and excellence but above all, it symbolises success and struggle. One didn't come without the other, and now I had joined the club.

When people see or hear your name, what do they associate it with? What are you known for? Have you found your niche in life? Make a name for yourself. It's your personal brand. You get dozens of labels throughout your life. Names that people call you are often uncomplimentary and downright derogatory, but you can reject their label and choose your own.

The Psychology of Performance

To succeed in sport, I knew you had to improve physically. Your stamina, strength, power, flexibility, agility, balance, and coordination are at stake. I also knew that you had to improve technically. What I didn't know was how big a part psychology played in performance. I still remember the first time that I had a conversation with a performance psychologist. Sitting on the opposite side of his desk, I paid lip service to the small talk and cut to the chase.

"Can you guarantee me a gold medal?"

"No."

"So, is there any point in me talking to you?"

There I was, denigrating his profession but his measured response surprised me. He had encouraged me earlier to talk a little about myself and at some point, I had mentioned the subject that I had studied at university.

"Aha, you are a mathematician," he said as if he had some sudden insight into something that could change the world. And he had. We saw the world differently. Mathematics is the antithesis of psychology, it is pure and absolute.

He knew that people show a tendency for a congruence bias, directly testing a given hypothesis rather than indirectly testing it. There was even a name for it in mathematics—proof by contradiction. But I was a non-believer, so he didn't try to lecture me. He just asked questions. He got me to analyse all the explanations that people give following a defeat. I related how they talked about having an off-day, losing focus, and lacking determination. They were all psychological explanations. I left his office wanting to know more, and I spent the next five years going back to university to study it.

So, what have you ruled out? What is the evidence supporting your point of view and equally important, what is the evidence contradicting it? Start a sceptic, finish a scholar. A healthy dose of scepticism isn't a bad starting point. We take in so much information without questioning its source or contemplating its accuracy. But rather than accepting and perpetuating assumptions, find out whether they are true or not.

The Binary Problem

For my Master's dissertation, I had researched how dieters think and behave. I knew only too well how obsessive the world of weight loss was from my time in judo. I had seen all the weird and wonderful ways that people tried to shed a few pounds so they can make the required weight before a competition. I skipped meals, sat in saunas, and even ran in a bin liner. I'm not saying that the things I practised were healthy, but I knew people who engaged in more harmful practices. However, dieting because of your body image isn't the same. Many people that I interviewed wore their weight as part of their identity. They perceived themselves and others as 'fat' or 'slim', irrespective of whether their actual body weight correlated with standard measures relating to body mass.

What really stood out for me though was the fact that the people who did achieve their weight loss goal were left with fragmented and incoherent identities. As part of their transition from 'fat' to 'slim', they often resented who they were and rejected their former self. Somehow in the real world, the division is never equal. It comes with the implicit assumption that in every binary system, one is subordinate to the other.

It is what I call the binary problem.

What is the one thing that you want to change about yourself? Is there an off-the-shelf solution to the problem?

It's hard to pinpoint the moment I became completely blind. The change happened gradually over a period of years, not months. But in all that time, there wasn't a day I didn't think about getting my sight back. I would visit the ophthalmologist every year, and he would deliver the same bad news, "Your sight is getting worse, and there's nothing we can do about it."

I was fixated on a solution that was out of my control, and it left me in a dark place, both literally and metaphorically. I didn't want to be blind. My stereotyped vision of blindness was of a piano tuner or a basket weaver. But I began asking the question how do blind achievers see their world?

I realised that true transformation only came when I was able to see blindness differently from how others saw it. I call it transcendence, the ability to see things from a level above and beyond the binary labels the world constructs for us.

As Albert Einstein once said, "We cannot solve our problems with the same level of thinking that created them." No matter how much we change, we must never lose the part of us that has given us the struggle. We can only incorporate more parts and abilities into our journey of the self.

D arren Harris is a dual Paralympian and a change agent who inspires others to see the world differently.

"Change doesn't have to reinvent the wheel, only get it turning in the right direction."

Not only has he studied the psychology of change, he has mastered it. He did so using his 20 years of real-life experience at the cutting edge of elite sport - competing in both football and judo, and winning 10 World and European medals in the process.

Darren provides tools, techniques and tips, as well as a personalised blueprint on how to master the art of self transformation in a way that ensures that success isn't just a one off.

Darren Harris
Website: http://www.darrenharris.me.uk/
Twitter: @DarrenHarrisGB
LinkedIn: darrenharrisgb

THE GOLDEN CHILD –
A TALE OF SELF-DISCOVERY
THROUGH THE POWER OF
SELF-DETERMINATION

DR. JERRY D. SMITH JR.

"The secret of fortune is joy in our hands. Welcome evermore to gods and men is the self-helping man. For him all doors are flung wide. Him all tongues greet, all honors crown, all eyes follow with desire. Our love goes out to him and embraces him because he did not need it."

- Ralph Waldo Emerson, Self-Reliance
and Other Essays

L ife is full of trials and tribulations. To be great is to face these things head-on with the knowledge that you may fail but with also the certainty that you will have left nothing undone that was within your power. You will also know that your efforts will lighten the burden of those following in your footsteps. After all, what is life if not the sharing of hardship and achievement with those we care for and leaving a legacy of overcoming barriers and obstacles?

And so, each individual's journey of self-discovery begins via the path of self-determination. In this chapter, I hope to share with you my story of self-discovery using the power of self-determination. Before I start, I want to point out there are numerous stories of what others have experienced that are similar to or worse than the ones recounted here. But this story is mine. It is a deeply personal story about my experiences and how I ultimately not only survived, but flourished.

I want to share it with you.

One of the earliest memories I have is of my father standing behind my mother in the living room of the two-bedroom trailer home that we lived in. One of my father's arms were wrapped around my mother, pinning her to him. His other hand held a pair of orange-handled scissors with the blades pointed at my mother's throat. My parents were divorced by now and my father did not live with us, but they still spent their fair share of time acting as if they weren't and he did.

My parents got divorced when I was around two years old, after returning from Greece where my father had been stationed as a U.S. airman. My mother and I moved to the small east Texas town where all my family was from. Over the next four to five years, despite being divorced and not living together, my parents had two more children together.

For years, my mother would ask me what I wanted for Christmas, my birthday, or some other occasion; I always responded with "I wish you and dad would get back together." I learned that my hope, of my parents someday getting back together permanently, was my hope alone. The adults seemed content with using me and my brothers as tools for hurting each other when things weren't going well between them. I learned that I could not trust my parents to put the needs of their children before their own. I learned that I had to look out for myself and my brothers and make peace with being geographically and emotionally torn between my parents.

My mother had official custody of all three of us. However, my father was frequently present in our lives—coming and going, as he continued his military life. Every other year or so, I would be sent to live with my father, wherever he was in the world, for a year. My brothers would usually just see our father a few times a year when he would stop by.

One year, my younger brother and I both went to live with our father in Germany. Throughout the years, there were comings and goings, arguments, and fights. I came to see myself and my siblings as pawns being used by my parents. They used us to hurt each other.

Then there was the sexual abuse. My recollection of the sexual abuse I suffered as a young child is somewhat sketchy. In part, I have always attributed this to not necessarily seeing what happened to me as abuse but rather just something that 'was.'

In my work as a psychologist, I have seen the confusion created by inconsistent messages given to young children about their sexuality. Mixed signals are common all throughout Western, in particular American, cultures. For me, I always thought of the unsolicited sexual contact I had experienced as a kind of childhood exploration and experimentation. A kind of childhood rite of passage, if you will.

I was molested (I use this term clinically) by two older male cousins when I was a pre-teen. However, because they were not 'that much' older, maybe older by 2–3 years, I did not see it as sexual abuse. And to some degree, I still do not see it as sexual abuse. I did understand that it was supposed to be a secret. So, on some level at least, I <u>did</u> know there was something 'off' about it.

This continued on and off for a few years whenever I happened to spend the night at their houses. I suppose that at some point we got old enough that I did not spend the night there anymore, and there was nothing that came out of it. On the other hand, I was sexually abused by another adult male cousin, an older brother to one of the cousins who originally molested me. This cousin had been charged with babysitting me and my brothers on several occasions. The abuse occurred a couple of times and continued until I became old enough to babysit my younger siblings.

Nothing was ever said about any of the abuse, and it was only when I was in my late twenties that my mother even indicated that she had known. This was only acknowledged after the same cousin was convicted and imprisoned for sexually abusing his daughter. In response, I casually acted as though I had no idea of what she was talking about. That was the only time in my entire life when anyone said anything about what had happened, except for when I chose to let a few select individuals know myself. This number now includes you, the reader.

Many people who have been sexually abused feel overwhelming shame and guilt in the context of what they experienced. Many develop life-long difficulties in coping with the world around them or developing healthy intimate relationships. Going through this experience, I learned to be constantly on guard and view the actions of others with suspicion.

My ethnic heritage is another area of relevance here. My father is black, and my mother is Caucasian. Until very recently, the family lore stipulated that I had Cherokee Indian genes from my father's side of the family and Choctaw Indian from my mother's side. With the increased popularity of DNA testing, I recently decided to gift DNA tests to several members of my family, only to discover that there was no Native American genetics on either side. So much for passing on the oral history of our people and our connection to the land our forefathers supposedly walked.

My earliest memory of becoming 'aware' of my 'race' was when I was about five or six years old. My white grandmother worked as a waitress at a bar in town. My white grandfather was a regular patron of the same bar, and everyone knew my mom's family. I'm not sure if it was a yearly event, but this particular year the bar was hosting a 'Come Meet Santa' event. The whole family, including two of my mother's sisters and their children, was loaded up in two or three vehicles and we all drove into town to join my grandparents at the bar and meet Santa. We were all so excited. When we arrived and joined the line outside the establishment, waiting to gain entrance, our excitement grew with each step closer to the front doors.

Eventually, my aunt and her two kids, who were ahead of us, reached the front door. They were greeted by an elderly woman whom I had seen several times earlier when my mom would bring me to the bar to see my grandmother or grandfather. After checking their tickets, she warmly greeted my cousins and wished them a "Merry Christmas" and motioned for them to enter.

Now it was our turn, my brother's and mine. We squirmed as we tried to contain our excitement. As my mother presented the elderly ticket-taker with our tickets, my brother and I started to make our way in to see Santa. Very quickly, the woman stopped us. "Umm…," she said directing her gaze toward my mother. "They can't come in here. No 'colored' children allowed." I remember being heart-broken as my mother took us out of the line, and we began to make our way back to the car.

While it is true that a child's mind can be fickle and that his recollection can be often questionable, I certainly do not recall my mother saying a word in response as my brother and I were barred from seeing Santa. It was as though she knew all along this was going to happen and had hoped that she would be proven wrong. But, what was even more hurtful to me, as a young child, was looking over my shoulder to see my aunt continue as if nothing had happened. She, without a word, gave her tickets to the lady and proceeded with our cousins into the bar, even as we left the line.

This scene has been stuck with me my entire life and has undoubtedly shaped how I've seen the world—now, and certainly as a young child. Through that experience, the child that I once was learned that the world is unfair, and no one will stand up for you. Not even those who claim to love you, if it means that they will have to sacrifice something. I also learned that sometimes those who we think will protect us are often powerless to do so.

Growing up bi-racial was difficult for me. I was once told by an older white man that I worked with that black people and white people should not be in relationships because their children suffer. He was correct, in part. Interracial children often did suffer. The implication of his words, however, was that since some people have a problem with interracial relationships, those who don't have these biases should make life less frustrating for those who do. I can tell you that interracial children who suffer only suffer because those who are prejudiced and intolerant would see the existence of such a child as the problem rather than see themselves as the source of the suffering.

When I was about 12 years old, I was at a large family reunion in my mother's (i.e., the white) side of the family. I was sitting at a picnic table between my two female cousins. We were voicing our observations of our family members, observations about the obligatory elderly purple haired aunt included, of course, when one of my older male cousins walked by. "He's fine," said my cousin on the right, "but he's got a nigger's butt." I turned to look at my cousin, who immediately asserted, "You're not black!" Embedded in her assertion was the idea that I should see myself as somehow better than the 'real' black people because I was half white, and so should naturally reject half of my family and their experiences as black people in America.

Unlike many of my friends when I was a pre-teen, I had friends who were of multiple ethnicities. As a pre-teen, I lived with my mother in the projects of Dallas, Texas. Despite the fact that the area had a relatively healthy mix of ethnicities, people tended to only associate with people of their own race/ethnicity. Poverty was the common factor with everybody living here. Although I personally associated with people from the Middle East, India, Africa, etc., my friends included primarily whites, blacks, and Hispanics. However, I never really felt comfortable with the two groups that made up my heritage. When I was with my white friends, I was 'the black guy'. When I was with my black friends, I was never quite 'black enough' and thus was viewed with some skepticism, if not outright suspicion.

As a bi-racial male, I never truly felt like I was accepted, regardless of whether it was with my extended family or my friends. I was always seen as something…different. This internal belief system likely began to develop as far back as when Santa lost his appeal for me. I learned pretty early on that people will always try to make you into a version of you that benefits them at that moment. They will do this with little to no regard for who you truly are. I learned that people did not want to know my truth.

When I was at the age of 11 or so, my mother started dating a man she met at work. Pretty soon, this person was living with us in our Dallas apartment. Later that year, my brothers and I went to stay with my father for a few weeks. He was now stationed in San Antonio, Texas, was remarried and had a four-year-old daughter.

During that summer, my father took us along to visit his sister, who happened to live in a suburb of Dallas. Since we were close to home, my father called my mother to let her know that we were at my aunt's and that she could come to see us. When my mother pulled up in front of my aunt's house, we were all in the front yard playing with a ball—my two younger brothers, my half-sister, and I. My mother grabbed my two younger brothers and told me to get in the car. Leaving my four-year-old sister alone in the front yard, my mother drove off. On the way home, she informed us she and her boyfriend were married. As her husband, she informed us, he was now our father and we would no longer have anything to do with our biological father.

As an adult, I would later tell my mother that "this was the day you died to me." My father showed up at our home shortly after we arrived and was greeted by my mother and "step-father" threatening to call the police and to kill him. After the police arrived, they advised my father that since he did not have custody of us, he would have to leave or risk being arrested. My father left, and we were left alone to face the systematic process that tried to eradicate him from our lives.

My younger brothers had never lived with my father for any extended period of time, and so they were quick to give in to the brainwashing of my mother and 'step-father.' It should be noted that our 'step-father' was not actually our step-father at this time. He and my mother did not get married until several years later, a fact that I happened across when I discovered their marriage certificate while I was in college. Nevertheless, we were told repeatedly that our father did not want us and did not care about us. This litany would later be upgraded to the tale of him not even being our biological father— our biological father being some unknown person who may or may not have been a father to all of us.

We were forced to refer to our step-father as 'dad' or 'daddy' and could only have the minimal food to eat unless we asked him and referred to him as 'dad.' Our biological father, if we referenced him, was supposed to be referred to by his first name, a name that I share. A name, as my step-father maliciously informed an impressionable 11-year-old me, that was a "girl's name."

Needless to say, it was not easy to persuade me that the only father I had ever known had never cared about me, didn't want me, and had graciously been replaced by this clinically-diagnosable narcissistic and antisocial personality disordered individual. As a result of my resistance, several weeks later my mother agreed to let me go live with my father permanently. It was this decision that started to break the bonds of my relationships with my brothers. After I left, there was no one there to stop the full psychological assault on my brothers; an assault that now included me as the 'bad guy' in the alternate version of reality that my mother and step-father cooked up.

A year later, owing to the failing marriage between my father and my step-mother, I returned to live with my mother, brothers, and step-father. Thus began the darkest phase of my life.

Over the next three years, from seventh to ninth grade, I would fall into a deep, though unrecognized and untreated, depression as I came to hate my mother and step-father. I grew further apart from my brothers, contemplated suicide over and over again, and joined a street gang trying to find the love and acceptance that I didn't have at home. It didn't help that I didn't much care for my biological father either. I viewed him as selfish, conceited, and emotionally distant.

I felt like I didn't fit in and that I had been abandoned by my family, so out of desperation and my social isolation, I joined a street gang. I was trying to find acceptance and a new sense of family, but it didn't work. Around my fourteenth birthday, I boarded a flight to London, England. I was going to live with my father again after things at home had reached a boiling point. By now, my mother had started to lash out physically at my continued resistance to the indoctrination.

Now, I had adopted a world-view in which friendship did not exist. I couldn't trust or depend upon my family, or anybody else for that matter; the only true thing in life was suffering. However, within that destructive world-view lay a seed that, unknown to me, had slowly been implanting itself. Waiting for its time to blossom in the sun. It had been there the whole time, slowly growing, fortifying itself, and preparing itself.

> "In the egoic state, your sense of self, your identity, is derived from your thinking mind - in other words, what your mind tells you about yourself: the storyline of you, the memories, the expectations, all the thoughts that go through your head continuously and the emotions that reflect those thoughts. All those things make up your sense of self." (from Eckhart Tolle's *The Golden Child*)

Because of all the tribulations that I had experienced in my life, I knew I had to find a way to not just survive, but thrive, psychologically. I knew that if I did not find some way of navigating through the depressive world that I was living in, I would succumb to its darkness. I knew all of this, but I just wasn't aware of my knowledge.

The first time that I felt the world reject me because of my racial makeup, a seed was planted. I envisioned an individual who could not be phased by this world's prejudices. I called this being 'The Golden Child.' I was to become this being. Initially, this moniker was simply a way of owning my racial identity. Throughout my life, people have continually asked me what my race was. By the time that I had made my way to England at the age of fourteen, I had begun to answer this question by stating, "I'm gold."

When prompted for a further explanation, I would simply point to the gold tone of my skin and say, "I'm a golden mix of black and white." Many people were amused by this. Inevitably, when a new person would encounter my circle of associates (I still refused to consider anyone a friend) and make an inquiry about my ethnicity, my associates would quickly speak up asserting, "Jerry's gold!"

As I began to assert myself in my own life, 'The Golden Child' began to blossom. Having experienced the emotional darkness and chaos of the world around me, I envisioned myself being in absolute control of my emotions so that I could never lash out to harm another being unless I knowingly willed it. I was determined that I wanted to be a person of reason and purity, to counteract the effects of all the unfairness and irrationality of my childhood. I became determined to be a being of love, having never felt that as a child. Acting on these ideals did not come easily because I continued to carry the pain of my past. Still, I was determined to be who I wanted to be, not what the universe seemed to demand of me.

As I committed to being these things, I began to look at various religious faiths to find a path forward. I studied all the world's major religions. This led me into a devastating era of my life that shook me to my core and destroyed who I thought I was. Having been raised a Christian, I was deeply rooted in my faith. (Faith, after all, is a sanctuary for many who have been abused and victimized.) I considered myself to be an intellectual and a scholar, so I had always intellectually known that religious belief is more a product of acculturation than a personal choice. However, I had never truly processed what that meant for me, as an individual.

After my sophomore year of college, I was staying with my mother during the summer. I woke up one morning with a sudden realization that if I were born anywhere else in the world, I would believe just as strongly in that culture's religion as I did in Christianity. It just happened to be the religion of the culture to which I was born. This was devastating to me, and overnight (literally) I became spiritually lost. I wandered in the wilderness of doubt and spiritual uncertainty for the next six years. Despite everything else that I had been through in my life, this was the most painful experience that I had ever felt. I blamed myself for somehow abandoning God and fell back into despair. I even jumped out of a perfectly good airplane in the hopes of having some kind of spiritual re-awakening.

It didn't work.

In 1999, my first child was born—a son. Over the next three years, I watched my son grow as I continued to try to cope with my loss of spirituality, the anger and hatred that I held toward my parents and my step-father, the pressures of attending graduate school while working full-time and being a relatively new father.

I was determined that his life would be as far away from the one that I had lived as possible. He would never experience the chaos, cruelty, and negligence of a child in need. As I watched him grow, I remembered the golden child that I was. I remembered that using that vision as a vehicle, I had survived my past, even if I had not yet overcome it.

On 7 November, 2002, as I was driving home from a graduate class, I decided that I was done with all the pain that I had been holding on to. I thanked The Golden Child for everything that he had done for me, and I freed him from his role as a protector. I forgave my parents and my step-father right there in the car as I drove onto the highway overpass joining Interstate 635 and Interstate 30 and made my way home to see my wife and son.

I had determined that my life from that point forward would be completely of my own choosing. Now, my son had become the fulfilment of The Golden Child's purpose for me. Every time that I looked at him, I recommitted myself to be the determinant of my future.

My story is not an uncommon one. It is a story of heartbreak, sorrow, circumstance, and self-determination. The difference between those who succumb to the darkness of their lives and those who rise above it, as I see it, is that those who rise up refuse to succumb. It's that straight-forward. We all have the ability to overcome life's trials and tribulations within us. The key is being determined to rise and being determined to overcome.

Self-determination is not easy, which is why so many people fail and ultimately do fall prey to the world's darkness. However, that failure is not always the result of a lack of available tools. It is most often the result of a lack of knowledge. You may not know what tools you already possess and how to put those tools to best use. Self-determination means taking an audit of the internal resources that you do have—that we all have—and then putting them to use.

Self-determination means not letting life's circumstances or the decisions of others dictate how your life will turn out. It means being self-reliant when you are the only one who can get you over the next obstacle. It also means being willing and having the courage to rely on others when there is a genuine need. It means having a healthy optimism about the promise of the future. You need to imagine the abundance that the future can hold if you only but put yourself on the right path to get there. It means showing resilience in the face of despair, pain, sorrow, and setbacks.

Above all, having self-determination means being willing to TAKE ACTION. You need to be able to take productive action to achieve the things that you want in life. All of these things that I had to learn and find within myself, you can, too. So, what are you waiting for?

D
r. Jerry D. Smith Jr. is a clinical psychologist, business consultant, and leadership development coach. He is the founder of Breakthrough Psychological Solutions PLLC (www.psychbreakthrough.com), a psychological consulting firm, and co-founder of Kara & Jerry Coaching (www.karaandjerry.com). Dr. Smith is ranked in the national Top 5 health care providers for improving relationships, in the national Top 5 for counseling practitioners. He was awarded the prestigious "Top Psychologist" award in 2015, 2016, and 2017 for the state of Texas, and was awarded the U.S. national award in 2016 by HealthTap.com. He has published numerous articles, and has been featured in more. He is a sought after expert in fields of mental health, crisis communication, negotiations, leadership development, and team building. Along with his wife, Kara, Dr. Smith is the co-creator of the Critical Dynamics model for building and managing high performance corporate teams. He lives and practices in Texas.

Jerry D. Smith Jr., Psy.D.
Licensed Psychologist & Consultant
Breakthrough Psychological Solutions, PLLC
30 Crocus Petal St.
The Woodlands, TX 77382
(O) 409-344-3581
(F) 972-692-7303
www.psychbreakthrough.com
twitter: @ClinicalPsychDr
LinkedIn: www.linkedin.com/in/jerrysmith32
Facebook: www.facebook.com/ClinicalPsychDoc

"I am the Storm": Standing Up & Standing Out - Learning to Do What's Right, Not what's Easy

JAMES WOODWORTH

Fate whispered to the warrior
"You cannot withstand the storm"
The warrior whispered back
"I am the storm"

Social Confidence Coaching through the Thrive Program
https://jameswoodworth.com

Prologue: The Most Inspirational Woman in the UK, and Me

"You have power over your mind – not outside events. Realize this, and you will find strength"

Marcus Aurelius

It's just after 1 o' clock on a warm, sunny day in May 2017, and I've just entered the room in which I will be doing my presentation, 3 hours from now. The room is creepily officious and more than a little intimidating. The raised, semi-circular seating is reminiscent of an amphitheatre, but I'm not in ancient Greece or Rome. The dark oak panelling and deep, red velvety cushioning on the seating makes me think of a court of law, but I'm not on trial; although some might think so, as I stand there waiting to walk onto the stage.

It's a few minutes after 4:00, and The Most Inspirational Woman in the UK (2017) concludes her passionate and punchy presentation; as she does so, there's no doubt in my mind as to why she received this momentous award—it's clearly well deserved. As the applause dies down, she introduces me to the audience and invites me forward.

I stand centre stage, facing the audience and adopting the speaker's stance—feet close together, toes pointing forward, hip wide apart. With shoulders back, I smile, take a deep breath, and pause. I choose a participant in the second row to my left. I look directly at her and say, "I believe resilience is a great skill to have. How many people here agree with me? If you agree, raise your hand and say AYE!" The enthusiastic response is unanimous. I continue, "I agree with you. Resilience is a great skill to have. Can we also agree on a definition of resilience? Yes or no? That's great. Let's agree on a definition. A common definition of resilience might go something like this: 'It doesn't matter how many times we get knocked down, what does matter is how many times we stand back up again, dust ourselves down and get on with it'. Are we in agreement that what I've just offered you is a good definition of resilience? Yes or no? Great, we're in agreement. Resilience or bounce-back-ability is a great skill to have, but here's the thing folks, what do you think is a better strategy: Strategy A: bouncing back from adversity or strategy B: staying on your feet during adversity. It's staying on your feet, right?" The response, again, is unanimous. "Bounce-back-ability" I continue, "is a great skill to have but I've got a better strategy for you, it's called thriving!"

I complete my presentation in 30 minutes. Everyone applauds, but it's the warm smile of the Miss Marple look-a-like, sitting directly in front of me on the second row, that will stick in my mind as I later recall that event. I smile and thank the audience for their appreciation. As I do so, I can't help but think of the shy, timid boy who would rather die than speak up in public—well, that's not entirely true, of course, but you know what I mean.

I'm also struck by the name of the charity whose annual conference I was speaking at. The charity is called FEARLESS. They encourage young people to say 'NO' to behaviours that deny them their values including the kind of behaviours associated with criminality, such as not getting involved in knife crime, gang culture and so on. They inspire young people to be fearless and to stand up and resist the difficulties that they are facing as young people—a noble cause indeed and one I was proud to be a small part of. It occurred to me that I had also learned to be fearless— not to say 'NO' to criminality, but to say 'NO' to the fear of rejection, to say 'NO' to the fear of uncertainty, unpredictability, the unknown, and more importantly, to say 'NO' to the refusal to change.

Liberation and Freedom: Escaping the Fear Prison

"Make the best use of what is in your power, and take the rest as it happens."

Epictetus

I'm curious to know, so allow me to ask you a question: how many of you, reading this today, have felt anxious in social situations? Being interviewed for a job, making a speech, doing a presentation, or asking someone out on a date are all the kind of experiences that people may describe as being more than a little bit scary. Wall-flowers and top nerds take note: it's perfectly normal to feel scared in social situations such as these! Research suggests, for example, that the number one fear in the Western World is public speaking, followed by the fear of death. This means, as Jerry Seinfeld points out, that the average person attending a funeral would feel better off being in the coffin than reading the eulogy. That's crazy! I know public speaking can be scary because we run the risk of screwing up and making a fool of ourselves. Now, I don't know about you, but I'll choose public humiliation over premature death every time; To put it more accurately, I would now but I might have thought differently in the past.

You see, I've got a confession to make. I can enjoy a whole range of social situations *now*, but the fact of the matter is that I used to be terrified of just about every social situation you can think of, including talking to strangers, speaking up at school, and of course… public speaking. And, I'm not just talking about doing a presentation or a speech at a birthday or a wedding. Being asked to read something out loud or to do a sum in front of the whole class would turn me into a stuttering, blushing, gibbering wreck of a boy. And don't even get me started on what it was like when I was trying to talk to girls! In fact, I don't think I even talked to a girl until I was 21, and when I did try … well, it wasn't a huge success, I can tell you that.

When you look in a mirror, what do you see? For years, what I saw was a timid, socially awkward boy who believed that he simply wasn't good enough. I really did struggle at school, but here's the thing: I may have struggled to do well at school, but only *socially*. The fact of the matter is that I've always really, really enjoyed learning. So, I knew that I could do well educationally because I knew that I wasn't stupid. In fact, I even knew the reason why I consistently failed to do well at school. It was because I was really, really shy! The amount of anxiety I carried literally stopped me from thinking straight, particularly in exams.

It wasn't just my schooling that suffered. The social anxiety affected my personal life as well. To be fair, I coped reasonably well—both in and out of school. But then again, that's the whole point. I learned to cope, but I certainly wasn't thriving! I coped by 'making do,' I coped by avoiding and playing safe, and I coped by saying 'No' to socially challenging events and experiences.

Then, one day, when I was in my late 20s, I made a BIG DECISION. I decided to become a teacher. I did this for two very important reasons. Firstly, training to be a teacher would enable me to learn everything I needed to know in order to conquer my fears once and for all (which, I'm pleased to say, it did); secondly, and most importantly, being a teacher would enable me to fulfil my 'why'— my purpose in life which, I realised quite early on in my life, was to *serve others*. I wanted to work with people and provide for them the inspirational leadership I wish I'd experienced when I was a kid.

You see, I didn't really want to teach a subject as such. Although, I did love my subject. No, the reason I wanted to teach was that I wanted to help young people identify and overcome the barriers that may have been preventing them from fulfilling their complete potential. Barriers such as a lack of self-belief, low self-esteem, and most importantly shyness and social anxiety. I was a teacher for 25 years, and I loved every minute of it. Then, I made another momentous decision. I left teaching in order to commit myself fully to the business that I'm involved in today—teaching people to *thrive in life*, which is something I now know I was doing all along as a teacher.

As of today, I'm continuing to fulfil my purpose in life as a social confidence coach; I'm teaching shy guys globally exactly what they need to know in order to truly thrive in life. I'm living the dream.

Choices and Decisions: The Moments That Shape our Lives

"It is not because things are difficult that we do not dare, it is because we do not dare that they are difficult."

Seneca

Making the *decision* to be a teacher was easy. Following through with a *commitment* and doing the training required was a lot more difficult. As I considered the options that were open to me, the harsh and punitive inner critic who'd been squatting within my head for years spoke out: *"Who do think you are—thinking you could be a teacher?" "What if you apply to teacher training college and they reject you?" "What if they accept you but you can't cope and fail the course?"*

Needless to say, I had a tendency to listen to the harsh inner critic that I had installed in my head. I gave in to the self-doubt that was so familiar to me from my childhood. The lack of confidence that would lead me to say things like *"If I try and speak to strangers, I'll experience rejection, hurt, and humiliation. I don't want to experience these emotions so I wouldn't speak to stranger."* or *"I understand that challenging myself to overcome social anxiety would be good for me, but the thing is that I don't have the time, I'm too busy. I'll do it some other time."* I remember making many excuses along the lines of *"I don't really want to be socially confident. I don't mind being shy and socially awkward. I'm alright with the way that I am."* And so, as I thought about becoming a teacher, I would talk myself out of it by saying things like *"You don't really want to become a teacher, do you? You're just saying that. You're happy doing what you're doing aren't you?"*

But the *desire, the need, the want* to be a teacher just continued to grow, whereas the potential pain of trying and failing was still there. As a fear, it was real enough but so was the desire to serve, to help others, and to make a significant *difference* to the lives of others. Gradually, the desire to serve began to overpower the potential pain of failure. I came to realise that successful people don't do what's *easy*, but they do what's *right*. Serving others was the right thing for me to do. I knew that I would never be truly satisfied until I'd lived my 'why'—my purpose in life. I also came to realize that the self-criticism to which I'd subjected myself all through my life wasn't true. I'd simply fallen into the erroneous habit of telling myself negative stories such as the "*You're not good enough*" story and so on. The stories that I'd been in the habit of telling myself were just stories. Stories, moreover, that were total BS! So, I made another BIG DECISION. I decided to stop telling myself crap stories about how crap I was, and I started telling myself some different stories instead. These stories would shape my worldview in a more positive way, forever. And with that, everything began to change.

The Path with the Greatest Resistance: Doing What's Right, Not What's Easy

"If you are distressed by external events, the pain is not due to the thing itself, but due to your estimate of it, and this you have the power to revoke."

Marcus Aurelius

I really enjoy presenting myself to people in a way that I did at the FEARLESS annual conference earlier in the year. I really enjoy telling people all about The Thrive Program, the Unique Branded Solution that I have for my clients—the UBS with no BS. People often comment on how confident I appear to be when speaking in public, where I seem naturally confident. I can understand where they're coming from because I certainly do enjoy coaching, training, and professional speaking. But as you now know, it hasn't always been like that nor has the path towards building great social confidence been an easy one for me. I didn't suddenly become hugely confident just by becoming a teacher.

Come back with me, if you will, to a warm, sunny day in August 2007. I'm standing in my kitchen. It's a large, brightly lit room facing the back garden that is bursting with life. The dominant colour is green, but there are flashes of violet. A deep powder-blue catches my eye, and a bright yellow, the kind that kids always seem to use when painting pictures of the sun, jumps out at me. Somewhere close by children are playing, birds are singing everywhere, and there's the strangely comforting sound of someone mowing their lawn in the distance. And boy do I need comforting!

I look down at an application form that I have just completed. It's ready to post, the deadline is nearly upon me, and I'm scared. I'm too scared to send it. "What if you submit the form and the application is rejected? What makes you think you can do this? Who do you think you are?" You see, the thing is that this was no ordinary application form. I was applying to study for a research degree at the University of Cambridge, one of the greatest universities in the world. Why on Earth would they want me? Who was I to think that I could study at such a prodigious institution? I was kidding myself, right? This was a few years ago now. And I was doing really well in my life. I was enjoying a successful career as a teacher, trainer, mentor, and coach, and I wanted to expand my career with further study, so why the self-doubt?

Imagine a teenage boy sitting an English exam, or at least that's what he was supposed to be doing, but all he's really doing is staring down at a blank piece of paper. And that's what he handed in at the end of the exam—a blank piece of paper!

That teenage boy was me, and I can still remember the anxiety I felt on that day. It was the same anxiety I felt nearly every day at school. I feared failing and making mistakes, I feared being hurt and humiliated, I feared getting things wrong, and I feared being rejected. Socially, I felt weird, awkward, and out of place.

Needless to say, my first attempts to do well educationally weren't a great success. You see, I was really, really shy back then. I had no confidence in myself whatsoever, and I created an unbelievable amount of anxiety whenever I was 'tested' or asked to present myself in front of others. I felt so self-conscious that I would avoid social situations as much as possible. However, that was a long time ago.

The Journey Continues: Focusing on the Horizon

"The mind that is anxious about the future is miserable."

Seneca

I'm an introvert by nature, and proud to be so, but the thing is that I'm no longer shy or lack confidence and I belief in myself. Now, I enjoy social occasions and social interactions, including meeting new people and speaking in public. All the confidence that I have now has also enabled me to enjoy a very successful career. So, what was the catalyst that encouraged me to overcome my social anxiety?

Well, as you now know, a number of years ago I made a number of decisions. I decided, for one, that I wasn't going to be scared and fearful anymore. I also decided I was no longer going to be socially anxious and undertook the task of teaching myself all I needed to know to have great social confidence, which I now thankfully possess. I taught myself how to overcome social anxiety, and my job now is to teach other people to do precisely that. I teach people just like you to have brilliant self-confidence and awesome self-belief, only it won't take you 30 years to learn what I learned. On the contrary, you can learn all that you need to know in just a couple of months using my program.

Oh, by the way, the University of Cambridge accepted me. I had no reason to worry. The thing is, as I learned to develop great social confidence, I also learned to succeed academically and professionally. The shy, timid boy who left school with hardly a qualification to his name went on to get a number of prestigious high-level qualifications. I became used to achievements and doing well. That said, applying to Cambridge was a big deal for me, and by far the most ambitious challenge I'd ever set myself. The self-doubt I felt as I questioned myself was a poignant reminder of the person that I used to be years ago. However, I did post the form, and not only was I accepted, but I went on to do well in the course. The shy person that I used to be ha been transformed into a humble and modest person who is, nevertheless, supremely confident.

I'm doing well in life and achieving many of the dreams that I've set for myself, but you need to understand that there's nothing special about me. I'm just an ordinary guy like you, and if I can overcome social anxiety, so can you. There's nothing special about me, unlike the strategies that I've got for you, which are quite exceptional.

Sometimes the hardest thing to do and the right thing to do are the same things. Our lives are neither determined by circumstance or the conditions within which we live nor by past experiences. They are determined by the *decisions* that we make. We need to understand that we always have a choice, until, of course, we make a decision; as soon as we make a decision, we cast aside any options available to us. The moment we make a choice, the choice becomes a decision. It was during several critical moments in my life that I made some important decisions, and it was in the moment of making those decisions that my life was shaped forever.

I decided to *stop* being socially anxious and to *start* being fulfilled; I decided to put an end to procrastination and self-doubt and to start getting clarity and focus on the direction that my life would take. In other words, I decided to take action—massive, constructive *action*.

The Choice is Ours

"Very little is needed to make a happy life; it is all within yourself, in your way of thinking."

Marcus Aurelius

What other people think, feel, and do is their responsibility, not yours. You're only responsible for yourself and what you think, feel, and do. You cannot control what other people think, feel, and do. You can only control what *you* think, feel, and do. When you take control of your *thoughts,* you can take control of your *life.*

You have a choice. You can give in to the pesky, little annoying thoughts that get you down, you can listen to the punitive self-talk that nags and bullies use to tell you off, you can give into negativity, pessimism, and the limiting beliefs that are holding you back, **or** you can take control of your life and everything it offers. You can start to take action, and you can start now if you want to. You can start moving towards the achievement of all your goals and aspirations.

Acting will enable you to get the great social confidence you've always dreamed of. The confidence that will allow you to assert yourself, to be bold, to be the high-status person you know you are. You can build a massive amount of social confidence, and as you do so, I'm sure you'll find your '*why*', your purpose in life, just as I did. The choice is yours.

Take Away: Your 30 Day Mental and Emotional Challenge: 3 Top Tips to Power up Your Social Confidence

"We are often more frightened than hurt, and we suffer more in our imagination than we do in reality."

Seneca

Now, I'm not sure if this is for you, but you've gotten to the end of the chapter, which is great. So, THANK YOU for sticking with me. I'd also like to show you my appreciation by offering you a really cool takeaway. I've got something that I just know you're going to love. So here it is: I'm going to give you a simple, no BS, 30-day mental and emotional challenge that'll enable you to broaden and build awesome social confidence. On completion of this challenge, you'll be kicking ass, taking names, and crushing it socially where ever you go. Sounds awesome, right?

But don't get too excited just yet, because there are a few things that we need to get right before you get started on the challenge. Firstly, you need to understand that social anxiety isn't *real*. It doesn't exist as such. It's a *belief!* You believe that you're socially incompetent, but that's not necessarily true. It's just what you think, and it's just what *you believe*. It's just a story you're telling yourself, and this story is something you can change if you want to. You get this, right? You're the author, remember?

Social anxiety isn't really a part of you like the colour of your eyes, your blood group, and your DNA. Social anxiety is a form of learned behaviour. It's an unhealthy and emotional habit that you've developed, and like any habit, you can change it. So, the first thing that you need to understand before you engage in the process of change is that social anxiety isn't true. It's just a *belief* and a limiting and disempowering belief at that!

So, why does the challenge last 30 days? This brings me to my second point. Well, for a start, I quite like the idea of sticking to a plan of action for 30 days. The length of an average month is not only easy to remember but the idea that we can be free of all pesky, little annoying thoughts, feelings, and behaviours that we have in as little as four weeks is quite appealing. I'm sure you agree.

Research varies on how long it takes not only to break a habit, but to form a new one. To be fair, it can take several months, depending on the behaviours that you're dealing with. But, if you can fully integrate a new habit into your life *and stick to it* for 30 days, then I can't see any reason why you won't be able to integrate that new behaviour *completely* into your life in due course. Also, you can't expect to conquer social anxiety by dabbling in change or by doing something scary a couple of times. You need a consistent and determined approach. This brings me to the third and final point: *commitment.*

It's really important for you to understand that breaking an unhealthy habit and creating a new, more beneficial habit has nothing to do with willpower. It's simply a question of *commitment.* It isn't willpower that gets you up in the morning to go to the gym, it isn't willpower that keeps your body in good shape, it isn't willpower that motivates you to volunteer to do a presentation at work, to ask someone out for a coffee, or to apply for a new job. It is *commitment.*

Relying on willpower leads to an internal civil war breaking out inside your head—a violent conflict between what you *want* and what you *think* you should do. This internal civil war will leave you feeling emotionally and mentally exhausted, and you're unlikely to be able to maintain the motivation that's needed to create and keep real, lasting change. *Commitment*, by comparison, is about taking bold, constructive ACTION. Commitment is a *state* of being that's wholly dedicated to the achievement of a goal. It represents an obligation that reduces the options and choices open to us and puts an end to procrastination, indecision, distraction, delay, denial and doubt.

So, here's your 30-day mental and emotional challenge:

1. **Employ a Supportive Inner Coach:** We talk to ourselves all the time. This internal dialogue or self-talk can be helpful, beneficial, and supportive. Any negative and destructive self-talk that we employ is just an extension of the beliefs that we hold about ourselves. You would only say "*I'm not good enough*" if this is what you believed. If you believe you're going to be rejected, then believing "*I'm not good enough*" serves a useful purpose because it will stop you from socialising, thereby protecting you from the potential harm that comes with being rejected. The social anxiety we experience exists as a constant reminder of what we believe threatens us. If we genuinely believed we were safe in social situations, our minds wouldn't create fear or the negative self-talk that accompanies it. As soon as we begin to challenge and change the limiting beliefs we have about ourselves and as soon as we start to challenge and change the self-talk that represents our thoughts and beliefs, our social anxiety starts to disappear.

   Do this every day for a month: Watch out for any limiting beliefs you may have about socialising, and watch out for the negative, destructive self-talk that accompanies these limiting beliefs. These beliefs include "*I can't talk to strangers. I'm no good with people. I'm hopeless in social situations.*" Get into the habit of challenging unhelpful self-talk and start changing it to something beneficial, such as "*If other people can do it, so can I. I can learn, improve, and get better if I put my mind to it. I can turn things around by taking positive, constructive action, and I can do that now.*"

It isn't the social situations we fear that cause us to feel anxious but the thoughts and beliefs we have about those situations. So, in order to overcome social anxiety, we need to change what we believe about the social situations we find ourselves in. The exercise given above will help you do that. Social situations aren't really threatening, but if we *imagine* them to be so, they will be so. And that's the whole point. If we *imagine* people criticising us, if we *imagine* people judging us harshly, if we *imagine* people rejecting us, then we will create fear. This brings me to the next part of the challenge.

2. **Engage Your Imagination**: The past is in the past, and what is done is done. We can't change the past. Worrying about past misdemeanours will do us no favours. The future is also uncertain, and we cannot with certainty what will happen in the hours, days, weeks, months, and years to come. However, we also need to understand that the future will almost certainly happen for us, so planning for the future is an activity worth doing. As we set ourselves empowering and exciting goals, we will find ourselves *imagining* what our life will be like when those goals come true. This is motivating.

However, we may also find ourselves imagining bad things happening due, in part, to the way that we view the past. Focussing on the past is unhelpful for several reasons. Firstly, we run the risk of equating the present and the future with the past. In other words, if shit things happened to us in the past and we focus on these things, then we'll end up assuming that shit things will happen to us again in the present and future. Not very helpful! Secondly, we need to understand that the strategies that we used in the past, the ones that kept us feeling socially anxious, were unhelpful strategies. So, we need to remind ourselves that using those strategies would be really unhelpful and we need some better strategies instead. Focussing on the past limits our ability to do this. Finally, focusing on the past is likely to lead to a 'doomed from birth' mentality. This unhelpful way of thinking leads us to assume that we are just the way we are and that there's nothing much that we can do about it, which is total BS!

So, we need to get into the habit of using our imagination in a way that helps us create a helpful, beneficial, and empowering way forward. We need to imagine good things happening, and we need to imagine success. Imagining what we want rather than imagining what we fear is a much better strategy. We need, in other words, to create a compelling future for ourselves.

Do this every day for a month: Before engaging in any kind of social interaction, regardless of what it may be, imagine the encounter first. Imagine the up and coming interaction in a positive, empowering way. Imagine yourself walking up to the person you've chosen to interact with. Imagine yourself standing tall with a warm, friendly, inviting smile on your face, and imagine the other person smiling back at you, welcoming your approach. Imagine presenting yourself with confidence.

Imagine people responding to you positively. As with step 1, you need to believe in your confidence. Don't wait until you feel confident before you act with confidence. Believe and then act, and you'll soon feel the confidence growing within you. Confidence isn't something you have, it's something you create. You create it through your beliefs. If your inner critic pops up to tell you that it's not possible, then tell it to 'Piss off.' Tell your inner critic that you're trying really hard in learning to be socially confident and that you're not going to put up his negativity anymore. Get your inner coach on your side, cheering you on, helping you to imagine the way you want your life to be. And, now, our third and final step, which is by far the most important step.

3. **Take Action and Do What Scares You:** Let me ask you a few simple questions: Where do life's opportunities lie? Where will you find excitement and adventure? Where are your going to have the most fun: inside or outside your comfort zone? Outside your comfort zone, right? You should understand, your 'comfort zone' isn't really your *comfort* zone. It's your "I'm a boring old fart" zone. It's your "I'm too scared to do anything" zone, and it's basically your "I'm not fulfilling my potential" zone. You see, staying inside your comfort zone isn't really comfortable at all. It stops you from doing what you really want to do, and it stops you from being the person you really want to be. I can understand why you would want to stay there because you know as well as I do that stepping outside your comfort zone is scary and risky. Are you worried about getting hurt if you take a risk?

That's right, you might get hurt, but here's the thing: you will never achieve your goal of being socially confident while staying in your comfort zone. You've got to step out, step up, and do what you know is the right thing to do. Don't do what feels safe, but do what feels *right*. And whatever it is you choose to do, whether it's establishing eye contact, talking to strangers, or just about anything else, you must stick to it. Don't give up just because you couldn't do it *immediately*. You need to keep going until fear no longer has the power to stop you from doing what you want to do.

People sometimes don't get this. They have a go, experience fear or failure, tell themselves they don't like feeling scared or that they'll never succeed, and they give up. They run back as quickly as they can to their comfort zone. This is the wrong strategy. We need to keep going until fear no longer has a stranglehold on us. You see, the thing is that we're conditioned not to like fear. Our tendency is to run away from it as soon as we can. We need to condition ourselves not to give in to fear.

This isn't about avoiding fear or failure; on the contrary, this is about embracing whatever experiences come your way. It doesn't matter if you fail, and it doesn't matter if you feel scared. What does matter is that you're taking ACTION. This, by itself, is hugely liberating and empowering. Rather than giving into fear, discomfort, uncertainty, and unpredictability, we need to say to ourselves "I thrive on fear! I thrive on uncertainty! I thrive on discomfort."

Do this every day for a month: Tell yourself "I can do whatever I want, and it doesn't matter if I experience fear. It doesn't matter if I fail because it's irrelevant. What does matter is that I'm taking ACTION to develop great social confidence, and nothing and nobody is going to stop me. I'm going to keep going until the job is done!" Remember, social confidence takes time to master. You need to practice, practice, and practice some more. So, in addition to engaging in some empowering self-talk, set yourself some daily challenges. Choose just one task each day for the next 30 days, and challenge yourself to complete the task. Whether that's establishing eye contact, saying 'hello' to strangers in the street, or simply making small talk, do these things whenever you can. Start small and work up. Remember, it doesn't matter if you can't do it at first or if you do it badly. The key here is doing it. Do whatever you want, and don't let fear get in the way.

And finally, tell yourself this daily for the next 30 days: I THRIVE ON DIFFICULTY. I THRIVE ON UNCERTAINTY. I THRIVE ON UNPREDICTABILITY. I THRIVE ON THE CHALLENGES OF LIFE. I THRIVE ON ADVERSITY. THE STORM OF LIFE WILL NOT DEFEAT ME. I WILL DEFEAT THE STORM.

I AM THE WARRIOR. I AM THE STORM.

J ames is a fully qualified teacher, trainer, coach, and mentor with over 30-years of experience working in the personal and professional development industry. As a licensed Thrive Programme Consultant and Trainer, James works with passion and commitment in helping individuals around the world build stunning social confidence. A proud introvert, James was extremely shy at one time in his life but has coached himself towards achieving great social confidence. He now teaches others to do the same.

Contact details
Website: https://jameswoodworth.com
Email: jqmes@jameswoodworth.com

THE POWER OF ONE

RUTH OWEN

B e willing to go where life takes you and you will harness the Power of One. What does that mean, you may ask? In a nutshell, it's an integrated and coherent connection between mind, body and spirit; all elements of what is essentially you are working in harmony to create the life you choose. It's really about paying attention to what your soul, or higher self, is trying to tell you. It means getting out of your head and feeling it using your heart and body. It isn't about linear or logical thinking. Too often, we rely on our ability to think things through to find solutions or the way forward. It's instead allowing that quiet inner voice to guide you. Let me assure you that, whether you call it gut instinct or intuition, we all have it; we just need to learn to listen more.

The journey from victimhood to self-discovery, to empowerment, and then to ultimate freedom or self-realisation is not always easy. The journey for every soul can be fraught with disappointment, failure, loneliness, heartache and even crushing defeat. Let's not pretend otherwise. Consider, however, the joy of knowing that you are fulfilling your soul's mission, that what you are doing in this lifetime on this earth is absolutely in alignment with who you really are, which can put all the heartache into perspective. It is your unconscious self's desire to shake and awaken you to your true power; it is up to each one of us to either accept the mission or face the consequences of our resistance to what life and our soul is asking of us.

You are pure energy in motion contained in a body that happens to be called, well, whatever name you currently have. But that's not who you are, it's just a label for convenience. At your essence, you are an infinite being. As we know, energy cannot be destroyed, but it can be transmuted and transformed into something else. This can be a source of comfort, for example, when we lose a loved one. What about the transformation of the energetic body that is you now into something greater *while* you are living? It's entirely possible and indeed probable because another scientific fact that we also know is that nothing stands still. Everything is in constant motion and transitioning into something else. A good attitude to have in mind whenever we are going through a particularly challenging or difficult time is that it can't last and it *will* change. Like that pop song from the '80's, if you're at rock bottom, isn't it worth remembering that "The Only Way is Up"?

Having lived through a number of fairly rigorous challenges, my experience tells me that such moments or episodes in one's life are there for one reason and one reason only: to allow your soul to grow. Think of growth as learning. If a child is curious about a flame and tries to touch it, what happens? The child learns very quickly that fire hurts if you stick your fingers in it and rarely wants to repeat the experience.

The same is true for the soul. It wants you to be constantly growing and expanding, so it will send you the lessons that you need to learn to achieve that. Sometimes, the lessons are ones that you'd rather not go through, but if you are *listening*, if you are paying attention to the *lesson* rather than the experience, then you don't need to keep going through versions of the same scenario. How many people, for example, repeatedly make the same 'mistake' in partnerships? They always seem to go for the person who is like the one before and the one before that, essentially rehashing the same kind of relationship. The cycle only breaks when the message is understood: choose a different type of person to love, but more importantly, learn to love yourself first so your perception of 'other' changes. You'll then no longer be attracted to the type of person you know will hurt you. A part of the process of any learning business is to let go of judgements about whether an experience is 'good' or 'bad'. It just is. The point is to get the point.

Neale Donald Walsch puts it beautifully in his children's parable *The Little Soul and the Sun*, when God tells the little soul who has been suffering at the hands of others "I have sent you nothing but angels." What he means is that every tough situation or person you encounter is there for your benefit, no matter how unlikely that seems.

We tend to judge others and then summarily condemn them for treating us 'badly'. By doing so, we limit ourselves to the restricted capabilities of the human mind and close off access to the higher consciousness that has no opinion about others and their behaviour because these things are irrelevant in the larger scheme of things. It is only by detaching your mind from the mental cacophony of blame and judgement and integrating such experiences with your awareness that you understand the fire lesson and no longer have a need to keep testing how hot the flame really is.

Of course, it might not seem like a great learning vehicle at the time but a crisis, when viewed in hindsight, is an opportunity to view that person or event from a different angle. If we approach our experience with a curious and learning mind and the question "What can I learn from this experience and what is the benefit of it?", then we can go a long way to moving up a level in the game of life.

So, you might be asking yourself now "If my soul came here for a purpose, what has that got to do with my everyday life here on Earth? Where is the relevance and connection?"

Good question! Let me also ask you a question. Do you ever have kind of weird 'coincidences' that make you stop and think? Like this one time when I was at the very tip of Africa, walking on a very small path along the spine of a rock towards Cape Point, where the Atlantic crashes into the Pacific, something peculiar happened. As we walked along (you have to concentrate; it isn't a big path and it's a bone-smashing fall into either oceans), I heard a familiar voice coming from behind me. Randomly, by chance, it was someone I knew quite well but had not seen for a number of years, and we had not even been in touch with each other in the interim!

It was an extraordinary 'coincidence', given that there were only a handful of people on the path at that exact time. I believe the reason I met that person again—whom I knew when I was married and living a different life—was to be reminded of how far I had come in re-establishing myself after a gruelling divorce. Sometimes you need a little reminder of your journey from time to time.

At other times, you just need to listen to the messages that your soul is trying to send you through your deepest, heartfelt desires. A good friend of mine had been working in the HR domain for years but had grown bored and tired of it. What she had wanted to do for a long time was to become a coach but because she was a single mum and had to rely on her salary alone, she dismissed the idea of a career in coaching as impractical and risky, which is entirely reasonable. What happened next though was a clear indication that she needed to listen to the message. She got fired from not just one, but two jobs within six months through no fault of her own, so she finally understood that the *reason* she was made redundant was to give her the space to set up her own coaching business, which was really her heart's desire. She knew that coaching was her calling and is now a successful businesswoman.

How does your soul communicate its messages to you? It might be a feeling, or a sudden flash of insight, or an inspiration. It might also be through events that happen unexpectedly, sometimes seen as 'coincidences'.

There are two types of coincidences: those that happen out of the blue, which you were not expecting at all and leave you amazed and maybe even incredulous. ("I can't *believe* that just happened!") Then there are the 'coincidences' or as Carl Jung called them 'synchronicities', which you design intentionally because you have a desired outcome in mind. Let me explain.

You see, before a human becomes 'aware', it's likely that that person will unconsciously experience what we talked about earlier.

When the soul decides upon the lessons that its human form needs to learn, it creates seemingly random events or circumstances that are interpreted as 'coincidences' but are essentially learning opportunities.

The point of these coincidences is to make the human part of you stop and think "Wow, that's amazing! How did that happen? Why did it happen?" Maybe you have asked yourself the same questions and concluded after a 'chance encounter' that you actually did need to speak to a certain person at that particular time because it was somehow beneficial to you. Now, this is where it gets interesting. The more aware you are of these 'magical moments', the more likely it is that you are in fact able to create your own synchronicities consciously.

In other words, *you* are now in the driving seat of your experiences. It's like you have opened a channel of communication with your soul, your spirit, your higher self and are no longer at odds with what the soul has in mind. You are in partnership with that unseen energetic element that is also you. Yes, you have to suspend disbelief (and how! We humans sure are sceptical!) and view the world through the eyes of your inner child—with wonder, awe, and excitement. You can start off with small engineered synchronicities, like finding a parking spot in the right place at the right time. If the will, intent, and belief is there, you'll see how often it works for you.

A couple of years ago I arrived horribly late for an international flight at a small regional airport in England. I miscalculated the time I needed to leave, so I could drive and arrive 10 minutes before my flight—the last flight of the day. I also had to drop off a hired car beforehand. It did not bode well for me. There was no one at the rental return place, so I just abandoned the car and ran all the way to the terminal building. As crazy as it sounds, I was convinced that despite all reasonable assumptions to the contrary, I would make the flight. The airport seemed abandoned. Everyone had left. There was no one checking boarding cards, so I ran straight through to security. The whole area was in shutdown mode, but I could see two operators putting on their coats in a back room, getting ready to go home.

"Hello," I shouted. "I want to get on this plane!" Bewildered, they came back out and started up the screening machine without a word of complaint. It was quite surreal; they helped me with my various bags. They even radioed down to the gate to ask for assistance in taking all my stuff to the plane. Not one of the airport or airline personnel objected or even made an observation about the fact that I arrived practically at take-off time and that the flight had clearly been closed. As I arrived on board, panting, everyone was sitting there, patiently. No one was cross or annoyed at having to wait for me. I collapsed gratefully in my seat, and we took off just a couple of minutes later. Yes, it was a bizarre event that could probably never be repeated, especially given how rigorous airline travel is these days. And yet, it wasn't that surprising to me. I had just felt, against all the normal odds, that I would be on that flight.

Synchronicity, as Neale Donald Walsch says, is a "convergence of Will, Intent and Experience"; it's an updated version of "where there's a will, there's a way" if you like.

Many years ago, I made a pact with whoever was listening: God, the Universe, my higher self, or whatever word that works for you. I had seen a house that I had fallen in love with and wanted to live in with all my being. It was spectacular, and I wanted other people to share in its magnificence. So here was the deal: if I got my dream home, I promised that I would give something back to others less fortunate so that they could benefit from this beautiful home too.

We got the house in spite of some tough competition. I remembered my part of the bargain and organised a day for families who had severely mentally and physically disabled children. I wanted to give the parents some respite and a chance to relax and to allow the healthy siblings some time to enjoy themselves doing healthy activities. Sometimes, in families that take care of special-needs kids, the childhood of healthy siblings is overshadowed by the condition of their brother or sister; sometimes, their needs are overlooked, and they don't often get to do everyday, simple family activities together.

So, we organised a day of fun outdoor activities at our new home: pony rides, a bouncy castle, an ice-cream van, hot dogs, burgers and an outdoor play area for the healthy kids. For the grown-ups, the ones who constantly shoulder all the stress and anxiety of life and death crises and constant trips to medical facilities, we had wonderful volunteers offering massage, reflexology, food and wine, and a relaxed environment in which they could meet other families in a similar situation. Quite often, they get so immersed in their own problems that they become totally isolated. On the morning of the event, we had 15 families coming in to have fun, chat and chill out. However, it looked like rain was on the way. I jumped in my car to get last minute supplies and (this sounds mad, but it came from the heart) as I drove along, I opened the window and yelled at the sky, "Are you kidding me? I kept my promise and now you're going to dump rain on our parade and spoil their day? I'm telling you right now, you'd better get rid of those clouds. I want to see sunshine and blue skies by the time they all get here!" I don't think I knew or cared to whom I was addressing this outburst; all I knew is that my heartfelt intention was for the day to be a success and for the families to have the best time ever. Half an hour later, we greeted the families in glorious sunshine without a cloud in the sky. You might call it a mere coincidence, but I believe it was 'coincidence by design' because I wanted it to be a sunny and happy occasion to the core of my being. The sunshine made all the difference, and it was a joyous day.

The next event was more of a lesson in understanding coincidences that are unconscious and the ones that I believe are the messages from the soul.

It was my wedding day. I had walked out on my fiancé five months earlier after the tempestuous relationship had gone on for six years. I'd had enough and was prepared to start again on my own with nothing. He had different plans. I don't think anybody had walked out on him before, but whatever the reason, he pursued me relentlessly for two months. There were constant phone calls, letters, those old-timey things called CDs, a car (the only one he ever bought for me in the 18 years that we were together), and the promise of a five-star safari vacation. Finally, I relented and we went on an amazing trip to South Africa, but I was still full of trepidation and wary of being bamboozled into something I was sure I didn't want to do. It was the holiday of a lifetime. On the plane back home, he announced that he had already booked a date for our wedding, even though I was still unsure, and gave me the choice of three possible churches as a venue. Talk about planning a strategy in detail!

Fast forward two months. There I am in my bridal-finery, in the car headed to the church with my sister, who was my maid of honour. Our father had passed away 8 years earlier and I had made the decision to walk unaided up the aisle. First, because no-one could have replaced my Dad and second, because I felt it unnecessary to be "given away" like I was some possession. I had struggled with my decision to finally marry this man ever since the plane journey back from South Africa, and I was still not entirely convinced I should be getting married at all. Added to this, there were heavy thunder clouds everywhere that day and the rain was lashing down relentlessly. I suddenly got an insight into what I should do. Call it a flash of inspiration or a cry for some sort of sign, but this is what I said to the astonished driver, "Here's the deal: if it's raining like this when we get to the church, you can keep going. I'm not getting out. But if the rain stops, it means I have to get out and marry the bugger."

The rain at that point was torrential. It seemed like I was going to end up in Galway that night, but at the very moment that we turned into the churchyard, the rain stopped dead. Immediately. Like someone had switched off a tap. I couldn't quite believe it myself. But a deal's a deal and so I get out, trying to avoid the muddy puddles. I stood at the entrance to the church but realised I just couldn't move. My knees were knocking together, I was alone and terrified, and I wish I had asked for a supportive arm to lean on. People were turning around, ushers were trying to encourage me to walk, but I was still rooted to the spot for several minutes. Then, all of a sudden, I felt as though I was being scooped up and almost carried forward. I started to glide up the aisle. My Dad wasn't there in body, but I never had any doubts that he was with us in spirit that day. It was a beautiful ceremony. The church was packed, and as we came back down the aisle there was a spontaneous outburst of applause, which was pretty much unheard of at the time. Frankly, no one could quite believe that we were finally married.

We came out into the churchyard and demonic black clouds crowded the skies all around us, making it feel like night had come early, except that there was one break in the thick darkness above us. A ray of sunshine shone down through the clouds, like a spotlight in a theatre. The *only* bit of the stage it was illuminating was the churchyard. Whilst there was blackness all around us, we stood in the sunshine chatting to our guests and looking for all the world like it was a glorious summer day. I remember noticing all these details with awe and took them as signs that I was on the right path. That somehow this was what I was meant to be doing despite my grave misgivings.

It wasn't an easy marriage, but then I always knew it would be a challenge. I had tried to back out of it, but it was as if I knew that it was something I *had* to go through in order to learn the lessons I needed to learn. Part of the purpose, it turns out, was to bring six wonderful children into this world. Had it not stopped raining at that exact moment, I'm convinced that they would not be here, and I would not have learned as much as I have so far. I recognised that this marriage was part of my life's mission, and so I was committed wholeheartedly to doing the best job I could as a wife and mother. Whatever circumstances you find yourself in, it's your job to find what your mission is and to follow it. No one else can tell you because no one else *really* knows what's in your heart.

Sometimes, we *think* we know exactly where we are heading and why. We have a fixed notion in our heads about what we want to achieve, what success looks like for each of us, and how we need to travel the road to this success. Sometimes the signs are obvious that you are on the right path and 'in tune' with what your soul has in mind for you; you meet the right person at the right time, and the perfect opportunity falls in your lap. At other times, you might begin to feel like you are swimming upstream and nothing is working; everything is hard work. This is the precisely the moment that you need to take a rain check and tune in with what that soul of yours is begging for you to do instead.

Have you ever thought that you knew exactly where you wanted to go but somehow got derailed? I often think about the time I was 22 and unemployed. I'd finished my degree and frankly, I didn't have a clue about what I was going to do. I knew what I didn't want to do, but that wasn't really helping. I started looking for jobs in PR because I logically thought that I had the skills necessary to make a good career in this field. I was outgoing, a people-person; I liked parties, and I was reasonable at writing copy. I got a second interview at a small agency in Newcastle, England. I had to take two trains to get there, and my super-organised Dad dropped me off unreasonably early at the train station. I sat down with a coffee and a newspaper, knowing that I had an hour and a half to kill. Out of the blue, a man walked up to me and asked me to help him find his destination and the train that he needed to take. Why he chose to ask me when there were hundreds of people around us was a mystery to me at the time. He was deaf and dumb, and it was a struggle to find out all the information that he was looking for. I indicated the train that he should take, but he still looked lost, so I took him to the platform that he needed to be on and confirmed the arrival time of his train. Just as I had finished my task, I heard my train being announced—at the far end of the train station.

I ran as fast as I could through the crowded station, reaching there out of breath but relieved, just as my train was starting to move. I had my hand on the handle of the door and was about to board the moving train, but a guard stopped me and told me that I'd have to wait for the next one in another hour and a half. I watched as the train pulled slowly out of the station with that awful sinking feeling knowing that I'd just blown my chances. I knew that it was a futile mission, but I went to Newcastle anyway and of course arrived unacceptably late. I didn't get the job and for a while I wallowed in my disappointment and asked myself why I hadn't paid more attention to the time while helping someone else. As it turned out, it was the best thing that could have happened.

After this failed attempt at securing a job, I decided that PR might not be the road I should be taking. I decided that what I *really* wanted to do was work in television. I set my heart on it and talked to a friend of the family who presented a weekly farming programme on local TV. He set me up for an interview with the Deputy Head Controller of the station. As it happens, the TV station was also in Newcastle! Off I went, full of expectation and joy that I was going to be doing something that I knew I would love.

"So, what exactly do you want to do in television?" he asked.

"Err, I don't know really. I just know I want to be in television." I replied. This clearly wasn't very helpful for either party.

"Then what I suggest you do is go and start at the bottom in local radio and work your way up." he responded.

It was the best piece of advice that I'd ever received. It gave me the motivation to stick to it, and it also gave me the green light to really go after something that resonated with me more than anything I had ever experienced before. It was like he had taken all my nebulous desires and channelled them for me. Now, I had a passion and a goal and I pursued both relentlessly.

I became a real pain in the backside for the local radio station. I was calling in every day, asking if I could come in and do any job at all on a voluntary basis. It took them three weeks to give in to my pleadings; finally, I was invited to help out in the newsroom for a day. I had no idea what contribution I could make in the newsroom. Quite honestly, I was a little confused. It didn't seem like a very glamorous way to start off in radio.

The moment I walked into the newsroom, I was sent out with a reporter to 'shadow' her and watch how she tackled the job in hand—from preparation for the interview to the types of questions that she would ask to how she would edit the interview for bulletins. I was completely and utterly enthralled from the beginning. I just *knew* that this was what I was meant to do. I loved doing anything that they allowed me to do and was just so thrilled to be there. I didn't even care that I wasn't being paid. That was the last thing on my mind!

Here is the lesson that I learned: when you find your passion and your purpose, it doesn't matter what the rewards are; the reward is the thing that you are living and breathing. It feeds your soul, and it is a message that the truly great thinkers of this world have reiterated in many ways, for millennia. Once you have that part sorted, the rest will follow.

Neville Goddard was a master of manifestation, and he understood (all the way back in the 1930s) that it wasn't just thinking about what you want that attracts it to you, it's the feeling of actually *having* that thing which ensures that you will have whatever you truly desire in your life. At the same time, rather paradoxically, once you have your eyes on the prize you desire more than anything, you have to let go of expectation. In other words, it is not up to you *how* your dream will be manifested. That's where the trust comes in. You find the thing that will put fire in your soul and love in your heart—and then you let go, trusting that it will be delivered.

Napoleon Hill said, "Whatever the mind of man can conceive and believe, it can achieve. Thoughts are things and powerful things at that. When mixed with definiteness of purpose and burning desire, they can be translated into riches." Now I'm not saying that I found riches in radio, because I didn't. But what I did find was passion, purpose, and fun en route to getting my dream job. Along the way, there were a whole host of synchronicities, like the news editor at the radio station suggesting after a couple of weeks that I should apply for a place at the National Broadcasting School in London. With his help, I got accepted.

Once I was there, the school put me forward for a job at the AA. We were doing live broadcasts on the state of transport for all the London radio stations. At the same time, we all had to go for a day's experience in a 'real' radio station, LBC. The station's transport correspondent came up to me that day and told me that I needed to make myself known to the news editor, which I did. A few weeks later, I got a call asking me if I could come in at 5 am the next day to do the 'train cancellation shift.' Of course, I said yes. Because even though it was not what I ultimately wanted to do, I knew that it was the way to get a foot in the door. I knew that if I played my cards right, it would lead to something better. One morning, I had just finished my shift and heard the daily editor ranting about the news desk secretary not turning up that day.

"Do you know how to type?" he barked at me.

"Yes, sir!" I replied.

"Well sit down here then and get on with it!" he ordered.

I did and it was the best move ever. I got onto the news desk shift roster after that and was included in the team that was at the sharp end of national newsgathering for the entire commercial radio network. I was in my element, and I didn't care that I was doing double shifts and working practically all the time. I was blissfully happy and excited to be doing what I loved.

Being in that state that athletes, writers and professionals from all walks of life often call 'being in the zone' or 'in flow state' opens up that channel of inspiration that attracts other synchronicities and centres you in what I call the Power of One state of being. That state of being is where everything is congruent and moving in the same direction.

I was at the radio station one day, looking downhearted. Greg, the man who I had first met on my day of experience at LBC, asked what was wrong. I was going to be made homeless in a couple of weeks as my landlord had decided that he wanted his house back. I was too busy to look for alternative housing, and I had nowhere to go. Greg cheerfully offered his spare room on the spot and became not only a very dear friend but my mentor as well.

As a result of being the news desk secretary, I got to find out about jobs coming up around the network and so within months, I was moving back north to start 'at the bottom' in local radio as a junior reporter. Yes, I was earning a pittance, half what I had earned as a freelancer. Yes, I was living in a pretty dismal place that smelled of cat pee and motorbike oil. And yes, I was working anything from 10 to 16 hours a day, but all that was of no consequence to me. I was having the best time ever. Two and a half years later, I was out on a reporting job and bumped into one of the reporters from the same local TV network where I had gone for my 'chat' about working in television. "Any jobs open at your place?" I asked him, more tongue in cheek than serious. "I'll enquire," he replied.

The very next day, I got a phone call from the news editor, at the very station where I had gone for my 'chat'. I did not know the editor and in fact had never met him. He promised me a job that he knew was opening up in a couple of weeks. No interview, no selection process, not even a face to face meeting. Finally, it was the extraordinary realisation of the dream that I had created after missing out on a career in PR.

It had been four and a half years since I had decided that TV was to be my calling, but I had been so immersed in the daily grind of honing my craft in radio that I had simply put my ultimate goal to the back of my mind. And now, seemingly out of the blue, I was presented with the golden opportunity to do what I had wished for, all that time ago. I was so excited and I couldn't wait to tell my parents. Instead of just phoning with the news, I had an inkling that I should see them in person. I arranged to meet them in a town midway between their home and my place of work. I told them about my extraordinary job offer. I am so grateful now I took that opportunity to meet up with them; it was the last time that I would see my Dad alive.

Three weeks later, after my first week as a TV reporter, I got the phone call. My Dad had suffered a massive heart attack in the middle of a restaurant and had died instantly. I remain grateful to this day for two things. First, that he did not suffer for long. Second, he knew that I had finally achieved my goal before he left this world. I was able to tell him face to face because I had listened to my inner voice. It was the same voice that spoke to me after months of ever-increasing misery in my marriage. Over the years, things had gotten progressively worse because my husband was a narcissist and a workaholic who resented the time and effort I devoted to our many children.

He was a bully who liked to be in control of everything. The final straw was when he walked out for six weeks, leaving me alone with the children and a list of tasks that he wanted me to complete for his business. The only communication I received during the whole time was a bullet point email asking me to tick off the jobs that I had done. Naturally, I was devastated. But as time went on, I found that not only could I manage jobs and children perfectly well, I was enjoying the freedom of not having to tiptoe around him while I did it, just so he wouldn't be upset or angry. It was such a relief for him to be absent! Over the years, I had gradually been worn down by his constant criticism of how I behaved, how I looked, or even what I said. I had taken my marriage vows very seriously and believed that because I had made my choice, there was nothing to be done about it. I had resigned myself to a life of emotional unhappiness and emptiness. I was in my mid-40s, and honestly I felt like my life was over.

My belief is that when you make your mind up about something that is already on the radar of your higher self, magic happens. My mother had come to visit me when my husband was away. She didn't like to come when he was there because he treated her with what can only be described as contempt. I had arranged to take her out for dinner during that week, but I had to cancel it because I was obliged to finish an urgent project for my husband (let's call him Dave). I rescheduled our night out for the last night of her visit. She and I sat in the kitchen that afternoon, and I remember saying to her that for the first time since I had married Dave that I could actually imagine a life without him.

Without hesitation, she replied, "If that's how you feel, then do something about it now, before it's too late." Something extraordinary happened that very night. As we walked to the restaurant in the rain I saw a man standing outside. Immediately, my antennae were buzzing. In my head, I was wondering who he was, where he was from, and why he was by himself.

He opened the door for us and said something in a foreign accent. Now I was really curious! He sat alone, but I was aware of him all throughout the dinner. The table beside us was occupied by French people. When I offered to take pictures of the group, we got into a conversation about where I learned to speak fluent French. I told them that I used to live in Montpellier, Southern France. When they left, the lone figure asked in a loud voice if he had heard correctly. I replied that I had indeed lived in Montpellier. "That's where I'm from!" he said. Within seconds, he had joined our table and we began to chat earnestly. When my mother left to go to the bathroom, I was overwhelmed with a desire to kiss this man, whose name I didn't even know.

When we kissed, it was like the universe had exploded in my head. At that moment, nothing else existed except for the two of us and I was utterly lost.

I was totally honest with him, and I told him how I felt. I was at a crossroads in my life and although married, I wasn't sure I wanted to continue to be married. He was unfazed, so I tried another tack, hoping he would see the light and run a mile. "And I have six children," I said. He shrugged (as only the French can do), implying this was no obstacle either. Flummoxed, I left the restaurant with my mother and spent a sleepless night wondering what on earth I should do about this or indeed if I should do anything at all. This event, I realised shortly, was designed and orchestrated for one purpose: to make me see that no matter *what* I did or tried to do in order to make the irascible Dave happy, it was doomed to fail. Nothing would change, and nothing I could do would 'fix' my marriage. Only by creating such a massive thunderbolt in my life, my soul and my higher self were able to deliver the message that it was time to move on. I had put that thought to the back of my mind for years, mainly because our children were all still so young, but this was an opportunity to see the situation for what it really was.

When something so disruptive and explosive hits you, you *have* to pay attention. As I mentioned at the beginning, the path you are meant to take isn't always going to be easy. In fact, the process of separation and divorce was the hardest thing I have ever done. There were times when I couldn't see any light at the end of the tunnel. All that I could do was get from one end of the day to the other in one piece. After three years of surviving torture using nothing but perseverance and self-belief, I could finally begin my life anew. I learned many things along the way; I will try to keep it simple as I lay them all down.``<u>Find your inner voice.</u>

Meditation, nature walks, or spending any quiet time alone is essential. Have faith in your own wisdom. Listen to the advice of others, but don't heed it unless it resonates with you completely.

4. <u>Let go of judgement and blame.</u>
    This is corrosive to any being, especially in judging oneself. Learn to separate yourself from attachment to blame, shame, and finding fault. It achieves nothing. When you can release these things, you will find it to be incredibly liberating.

5. Let go of expectations.

The tendency of the mind is to want to control events and outcomes and to look for certain 'rewards' for effort. However, it is no match for the vastness of the universe with its infinite possibilities. Try to stay in the present, and do the best that you can at each given moment.

6. Forgive.

It has been scientifically proven that forgiveness is a powerful tool that can release us from past traumas. At **40 Years of Zen** in California, clients are taken through a process that allows them to forgive past events and people who have harmed them. One man worked for weeks, trying to forgive his older brother who had abused him as a child. Out of the blue, his brother, whom he hadn't been in contact with for a number of years, wrote to say how sorry he was for what he'd done. Often, the person we most need to forgive is ourselves.

7. Be Grateful.

The more grateful and appreciative one is for even the smallest of things, the more we have of the things that make us happy. Esther Hicks says that if you can maintain a happy thought for 17 seconds, it triggers the law of attraction into bringing more of it to you. "What you think about, you bring about", so stay as positive as you can. Appreciate all the good in your life.

8. Question Everything.

There is meaning and connection in everything; we just need to learn to look for it. If you bump into a 'coincidence', what is it trying to tell you? If you're faced with a seemingly insurmountable problem, what is the message behind it? Most of all, question yourself. What are you here to do? What gifts do you have that need to be shared with the world? We do all have gifts, and we are all here to make our own contribution in whatever way we can. There is a learned art to living your best life. We are all still in kindergarten in terms of understanding how to harness the magic and magnificence of life, but if we can pay attention to what our higher self is asking of us and combine it with heartfelt passion and the will to see it through, we shall see the Power of One in action.

R uth read French and German at Durham University in the UK, chiefly because she wanted to travel and live abroad. She qualified as a broadcast journalist, working in radio and television in the UK, before moving to the Caribbean to work for a publishing and promotion company, where she produced guides and videos for tourists. Following that, she was employed by a travel company to recruit and train personnel for the tourist industry. When she couldn't find any actor to play a "pirate wench" on a Spanish galleon that was running trips, she stood in as a pirate for six weeks!

Ruth lived in Ireland for 22 years, where she and her husband raised six children and dozens of horses. They travelled the world and split their time between Ireland and the Caribbean. After her divorce, Ruth went into business in Dublin, creating a successful French bakery, before relocating back to England.

In 2016, Ruth undertook an expedition to Antarctica with Robert Swan, who was the first person in history to lead expeditions on foot to both the North and the South Poles.

Recently, she got qualified as a Master Certified Trainer with Mindvalley, the online self-development and education platform, which aims to redefine education worldwide and reach a billion lives.

She now facilitates seminars for Mindvalley, and is a speaker and coach to women who want help in reclaiming their self-identity after divorce and separation.

Contact details:
Ruth Owen
Email: ruth6owen@gmail.com
Tel: +44 7949 444 871
FB: facebook.com/ruthowen.4
Website: TBA
LinkedIn: being updated

There MUST be a Way!

BRIAN PETERS

When I was only 11 years old and playing 'Simon Says', I discovered a breakthrough mindset that continues to affect and shape my life today in incredible ways. Of course, I hadn't known what had happened. It became clear only as I got older. I had discovered a success mindset that guided me to incredible successes and breakthroughs even through the darkest of times.

"Look at him."

"Look at her."

"They are doing really well."

"Did you see what they've got?"

"Have you heard about so and so?"

When I was growing up, this was a normal conversation at home. It was always as if 'the other people' had it all figured out, were successful at it, and knew how to do it. It was slowly ingrained in me that great things and great achievements only happened to other people. We 'just didn't know' and 'it wasn't our place.' We were never exposed to really going after something because there was no point. This subsequently allowed a style of thinking where I was inadequate because 'I didn't know' and 'everyone else was smarter than me.'

My experience resonates with what probably every one of us has gone through several times over something or the other. How often have we felt totally inadequate, unprepared, without the knowledge or experience or information? We have wondered which path to take, which career to choose, or which job to take. How do we know what decision is right in certain situations or areas of our life? How do we decide then? Is there a formula that tells us what to do? Is there a way? Let me tell you about how I found mine.

Like most children, I loved to play football in the park on Saturdays and Sundays. After school, I would be getting on my bike and going for rides and playing games whenever I could. I loved sports. Once, when I was 11 years old and just about to enter the secondary school, we were playing 'Simon Says' in the hall. For those who have never heard of this game, it's a game where the teacher has the kids running around a sports hall calling out commands. These would be such as 'Simon says stop', or 'Simon says sit down', or 'Simon says put your hands on your head'. If the teacher simply says 'sit down' and you sat down, you were out. The teacher hadn't said 'Simon says sit down'. The idea of the game, like every other, is not to be 'out'.

I loved winning all games, and I almost always won this game. Unfortunately, on this particular day, I had lost the button on my shorts, and as I was running around I could feel that if I put my hands up I was in danger of losing my shorts, so I had to make a mistake on purpose. So, I was out, and there were only three others left. As I was sitting down, I can distinctly hear myself say to myself, "I would love to do PE all day". I can also very clearly remember thinking to myself, "somebody must do PE all day, I know, I'll be a sportsman."

Coming from an environment where I was made to believe that achievement and great things always happen to other people, I distinctly remember hearing myself thinking, "I'm not good enough to be a sportsman, but somebody must do PE all day." Then I heard myself say, "I know, PE teachers do PE all day. I'll be a PE teacher!" At that time, I didn't feel I was smart or clever, but I sensed intuitively that there must be a way. I knew I would have to go to college. Who me? Yeah right! Other people achieve, not us. Nevertheless, from then on, whenever anyone asked me what I wanted to do when I grew up, I just stated 'be a PE teacher.' Ten years down the line, I was a qualified PE teacher.

Though I hadn't realised at the time, that round of Simon Says gave me something that would affect my life in incredible ways. What I had accidentally discovered was that if there was something that I absolutely wanted to do and achieve, I would unintentionally hear myself think 'there must be a way.' While this belief allowed my achievements to break through in the face of other people's doubts, the one thing it did for me was to bypass absolutely any doubters, INCLUDING MYSELF!

These moments have occurred to me throughout my life. I'm sure these have happened in your life as well, and some of you may be facing it right now. When you want to achieve something or take a different direction, you are filled with doubt and uncertainty. You feel you don't know how to go on. Your belief that there must be a way can be a beacon in the dark. However, simply saying 'there must be a way' with something you are only mildly interested in will have negligible effect. This is like expecting someone who is curious about a Rubik's cube and knows 'there must be a way' would be able to figure it out. In reality, they can't be bothered to figure it out as it'll make no difference to his life. What I'm saying is that there is an incredible power in 'there must be a way' when you have a burning desire to be and to do and to have and achieve, which will propel you to heights of achievement. This is especially true when what you want has either never been done or can be completely reinvented.

Like all people, there are things in life that we know would be a game changer for ourselves if we achieved them. Whether it's a sporting achievement, financial success, academic success, family achievement, or anything else. When you find that 'Thing' you deeply believe is something that 'has to happen', you are on the right path. When these moments came, I found myself bypassing many of the usual 'I can't do that, I'm not good enough, I don't know how…, no one has ever done that before' and the myriad of things we say to ourselves and hear from other people. I could hear these phrases in the back of my mind. Once I'd latched onto this thought, I knew with every fibre of my being that I had to do it. I could hear myself saying 'there must be a way.' It was as if a huge cloud of belief engulfed me and covered me with belief and certainty. It was firm and powerful in my ears, and I felt rock solid in my chest and gut. I knew I didn't know how 'yet', but I knew there must be a way and I would find it. There was absolutely no doubt in my mind.

So how has that belief helped a boy from a council house retire at the age of 38, become Mr. Universe, have a beautiful home close to the beach with a swimming pool, a tennis court and a purpose-built gym, and travel much of the world? Did I have my challenges? Absolutely! Serious ones? You bet. Potential dream killers? Without a doubt.

In my late teens, I was a top-flight badminton player. This meant I needed to be slim, light, and fast. So, my training involved many hours of running for endurance, sprints, and specific speed exercises on a badminton court. I 'knew' I didn't have special racket skills yet, but I also wanted be one of the best in the country. So, I heard myself say 'you may be able to outplay me, but you'll never be able to outlast me.' This was my strategy to answer the question I asked myself 'there must be a way I can be at the top.' Badminton can look like a fairly soft game when viewed on the TV or in the local recreation centres; however, at the top level, it's a war of stamina. Not only do you have to move incredibly quickly, you may have to do this for an hour. Added to that, tournaments often last all day. It can get down to the 'last man standing' type of thinking. You have to win matches throughout the day to get to the final. Sometimes, these matches may happen late in the afternoon or evening. This means you have been playing for hours. As one of the main tactics in badminton is to simply run your opponent into the ground, stamina and speed are vital.

I knew I wanted to be at the top. So, I figured out that as I developed my skills to the highest level, my answer to the question 'how I can make sure I can outlast and outrun everyone I meet in a tournament?' was 'There must be a way.' I just hadn't found it yet.

I created and developed the most insane training regimen for myself. After a period, I knew that anyone may be able to outplay me but never outlast me. The top players earn recognition by participating in all minor and major tournaments throughout the country. I was known for my skills and for being tireless; you had to bring it if you wanted to beat me. It was at this time that I came across a magazine featuring a Mr. Universe on the front and I was blown away. There was that moment of connection where my whole body and mind just knew that I had to look like that and be Mr. Universe. At that time, I was skinny and weighed 85 kg. It was the same intensity of connection I felt when I was 11 years old and wanted to be a PE teacher. I was so excited, and this thought was buzzing in my brain for days and weeks. I started incorporating weight training into my badminton training regimen, thinking it wouldn't look so bad to be a muscular badminton player. However, my passion to be Mr. Universe was overriding everything. It soon engulfed me.

I believe any top sportsman, businessman, or achiever will tell you that their desire moved from 'I would like that' to 'I can't afford not to.' This is a game changer. Its importance is so deep that you will ask yourself the question 'There must be a way.' Your perseverance will lead you to the answer.

For those of you unfamiliar with the real intricacies of bodybuilding, the results look great, but the path is hard. The average bodybuilder has no idea what it takes to be the number one in the world. Many bodybuilders like to look good in their local gym or down at the local bar with their mates, all assuming they could be a Mr. Universe if they wanted to. To win the title, you will have to be a champion of your country. You'll be competing against the best from the other countries. This is the ultimate 'big fish in a big pond' moment.

When you are dieting for a bodybuilding show, you need to achieve body fat levels as low as 3%. To achieve this, you must eat a lot of low-energy foods. This includes food with low carbohydrates, fat, and sugar. They give energy, and you have to cut them out or go real low and focus on protein foods to maintain muscle. Protein foods give very little energy. For example, if you eat steak for three days and nothing else, you will feel like someone has 'pulled the plug' on your energy. Now, do this for weeks and months at a time. If you have no willpower, there will be no title. To put this in perspective. When your energy level is this low, it takes 10 minutes to get the energy to even think about going to the bathroom, let alone train. This is the way to get the body fat down. Is it easy? No. Is it worth it? Absolutely!

For two years, everything I ate was weighed; values of protein, fat, carbohydrates and calories were recorded. Knowing that 'there must be a way' gave me the motivation to commit and follow through. This desire that you may have is just 'new.' You don't know how to get there, you don't know what to do, and you don't know what it takes. That's fine. Because if this is so important to you that it simply has to happen, you will find yourself saying 'there must be a way.' The challenge I had was that I was working in a job that really couldn't pay the food bills for a bodybuilder and allow the time to train full time. If you can't eat large amounts of food on a regular basis, take up golf. This journey costs money. I would meet my future wife just at this time, and she was a financial consultant. A year later, I joined the industry. I loved teaching and hated being poor. I was working long hours, earning good money, training when I could, and it became clear that I could be good at both. I didn't want to be good; I wanted to be great!

As John D. Rockefeller said, "Don't be afraid to give up the good to go for the great." I figured out that to achieve my sporting dream, I needed both money and time. I needed time to be able to just train as a full-time athlete and not worry about money. With my current setup, that was not going to happen. I heard myself say 'there must be a way.' What I came up with was a very risky move and decision. I decided I would become a top salesperson, work for a number of years, save enough money to be able to retire, and concentrate on bodybuilding full time.

Why was this risky? Most top bodybuilders win their big titles in their 30s. I was already 30 and a salesperson working 12 to 14 hours every day. I calculated that if I retired when I was 38, I would still be young, strong, and fit enough to be able to train and achieve my dream. That was my way. It was a risky move for numerous reasons. What if I didn't retire at 38 with enough money? What if it took longer to retire and I was going to be old? Could I pick up bodybuilding full time at 38 and still achieve my desire? There were numerous questions like these. Many times, you read the phrase 'follow your passion.' My passion was to be Mr. Universe. I couldn't just drop everything and become a bodybuilder because I couldn't afford it. I had to take a detour to follow my passion. Once I decided that this was the way, I never doubted the outcome.

Then came another challenge, how do I become the best sales person I can be and get the results I need?

Let me take you back to my original career. I was a teacher on a salary. I had a job for life. Now, I'm in a commission-only, no-result-no-money career that I had no clues about. This was all new and scary. I'm in a completely new learning curve all over again. Anyone in sales will tell you that commission-only sales are hard, especially at the beginning. Now let me correct that: it is terrifyingly hard. For me, it was terrifying. I'd gone from being liked and being in a respected position with hundreds of kids looking up to me to someone at the bottom of the pile who hasn't got a clue or a steady income. Plus, selling insurance doesn't exactly put you top of people's Xmas card list. I was completely out of my comfort zone. I'd gone from knowing all about my chosen career and skill area to not having a clue. Anyone making changes in their lives and careers will understand this.

After a few months in this new job, I could clearly see the challenges. There was the creeping fear that my sporting dream was drifting off elsewhere. However, I persevered. Through sheer grit and fear, I committed myself wholeheartedly. I also managed to earn some money in the first 5–6 months. In the next year, through hard work and relentlessness, I became the number one consultant in a company of 4,000 salespeople. Sounds good, doesn't it? Looks like I was having fun and success at the same time. Did the future look guaranteed? The truth is, it was tortuous and horrendous. Apart from selling and trying to pay the bills, the main part of the job was getting names and numbers of the friends of clients that you had managed to take on. I would have to later ring them up to ask for an appointment to sell them insurance, pensions, and savings.

The system was to collect as many names and numbers as you could during the week. On Friday afternoons, the whole office would call them and make appointments for the following week. I read many books on cold calling and telephone calling. And let me tell you, no one likes it. Almost everyone hates it. When people are saying 'You'll get used to it', don't believe them because they are lying. This is like someone saying, 'you will get used to poking yourself in the eye with a chopstick.' Well, trust me you won't.

We were taught strategies to get names and numbers at the end of a client meeting, and we were practicing them. For me, it was the same mental battle almost every time. I hated it and was absolutely terrified of the Friday calling sessions. Every Thursday, I felt like I was on death row and tomorrow was the day. If I chickened out, (which happened more than once) I would get momentary respite from the nightmare of calling. After this, I was worried over the weekend about the appointments. There was also the added pressure of being the No. 1 sales guy. My life was a day-to-day battle of wills with mental pain and torture. The sunny days were few and far between. What had I done? How could I have been so stupid to believe I could do this? I was in a doubt if 'I could do this' or 'I could last'; then I could see my dream disappearing past the universe and out into the cosmos.

If Anne-Marie ever reads this, you know I mean it when I say how much I'll always thank you and never forget your help. Despite being the top guy, I was terrified on Fridays. Anne-Marie, the deputy manager, would sit with me in a private room while I did my calls, to give me some support to encourage me or should I say give me courage because on Fridays I had very little of it. Every week I was going to quit either Thursday or Friday.

I was disgusted at my own weakness. I would lie in bed at night unable to sleep, and the fear of the next day would be running through me. Here I was, this ex-professional teacher in good shape, the number one consultant in a company of 4000, and I was supposed to have it together and 'know.' In reality, I was shaking like a leaf on Fridays and was terrified to pick up the phone. I used a private room to make calls as I was ashamed. So, Anne-Marie, an everlasting note of gratitude for your support.

Oscar Wilde said, "What seems to us as bitter trials are often blessings in disguise." At that moment, whatever blessings were hidden here were so well hidden that I could see only bitter trials.

The answer to the nightmare was referrals. When I looked at getting referrals, my whole brain and body were exploding with the thought 'there must be a way.' I was desperate at this point. I just had to figure it out if I was going to achieve my dream or even survive this business. Then must be a way to do this so I am not terrified every week. I knew that I just could not continue with this. There was no way I was going to be able to do this for a year. I just had to do it differently. So, I undertook the challenge and said to myself with utter conviction 'there must be a way.' I had to take these chopsticks out of my eyes.

To put this in perspective, imagine this: Every day, there are sales meetings across the world. In every sales meeting, every convention, every group training session, regardless of what sales skills are being taught, the number one question, without doubt, is always 'How do you get referrals?' The problem was, and is, the most pressing problem for many salespeople today. No one really knows or knew how to get referrals. So, there was no one to ask, copy, or follow. I had to find the way. I am not talking about an odd few referrals here and there by accident. I am talking about a systematic way to ensure referrals were arranged every appointment, by the day, week, month, and year. Almost anyone can sell to a certain degree. Even if you are unskilled, hanging around long enough enough you will be able to make a sale. I had no intention of starving, so I needed to figure it out. My whole sporting dream was now dependent on me finding the way.

I spent hours every night and every weekend trying to figure it out. I was trying to work out how I could get referrals from clients in a way that they were happy, so they would even call the client and introduce me while I was in the meeting. This hadn't even been heard of then. To find a way to do this successfully, with no mental battles with myself or fear of a battle with my clients, I started with the end in mind.

How can I get my client to want to introduce me to 2, 3 or even 4 other people? 'There must be a way.' I spent hundreds, subsequently thousands, of hours studying processes, systems, and the human psychology. I finally came up with a unique system that solved my referral problem. Not only did I then become the number one consultant every year for eight years and retired on time, I moved to the beach in a house with huge grounds, a tennis court and swimming pool. I later had a gym built. Did the solution come easily? Far from it. I would wrestle constantly with the problem and then there were 'aha' moments that moved me closer to the solution.

Einstein said, "The only valuable thing is intuition." I don't believe intuition just happens with no input. I absolutely believe that when you keep piling more and more information and desire for a solution into your conscious and subconscious, it works hard to figure it out. When it happens, 'aha' moments are created. Einstein further wrote, "I believe in intuition and inspiration… At times, I feel certain I am right while not knowing the reason." As my solution is unique, I didn't have anyone to follow. I had to have the belief that I was right, market-test it daily, and refine it if required. I worked it out. I found the way to become successful in my career and enjoy the process instead of wanting to slash my wrists almost every day. Anyone who is having a tough time in sales will know what I am talking about. Until I found the solution, it felt like I was in Dante's Inferno of Hell every day and every week.

I now have a very successful mentoring consultancy that helps salespeople in numerous markets solve their number one problem. Companies around the world now hire me to mentor their salespeople on how to get referrals and grow their businesses. I help solve their number one problem in sales: How to get the next client.

Had I not been absolutely committed to the outcome, the goal, and utterly convinced that I could find the way, I sincerely doubt I would have achieved any of the things I have today. Remember, at this stage, it is blind belief and faith driven by an absolute passion to achieve. This is all about finding the way.

Once while training for my bodybuilding competitions, I played a game of badminton with a long-time friend and snapped my

Achilles heel. Great! Now, what does my dream look like? A huge setback and months of recuperation after a delicate operation. As I was hobbling around on crutches in plaster, the same friend of mine asked me if I was still going to train for my competitions. This was an obvious question, and I responded saying "Of course." He then put me on the spot and asked how I'd do it.

I said I would do thousands of repetitions with a lightweight if I had to. I will find a way. The goal would not diminish. I had to assess the 'how.' I knew deep down there would be a way, I just had to find it! This was yet another example I underwent to where I had to 'change the route' in order to achieve my goal. The goal for which I worked hard for 8 straight years. The goal for which I had built up the necessary financial security.

During my preparation, I also felt I needed help. I was treading into unknown territories. I was my country champion and European champion, so whom do I talk to? This taught me that we should ask for help at the right time in certain phases of our life. It's obvious that top sportspeople have this figured out. In tennis, for example, the top players always have a coach behind them. Why need a coach if you are number 1? Simply because that's how you get to the top and stay at the top.

An extreme example of reaching out happened every year in Singapore, where I worked for a number of years. Every year, Warren Buffet auctioned off a lunch with just himself to the highest bidder. The money went to charity. The usual, and I use that word lightly, 'donation' to win the two-hour lunch was always in the region of $2 million. I am sure they got some 'insight' that propelled their business.

Even at the top of my own sales career, I was always searching to be better. I was always told myself "There must be a way I can be better, earn more, and be better with my time." I flew a sales coach over from the States to try to learn 'what didn't I know.' After all, we don't know what we don't know. He had written numerous books, so I gave it a shot. I learned that I was, in fact, more highly skilled and knew a lot more than this guy, and earned more than he did. However, I got one new question that I could use in my business and the confirmation I was good at what I did. This one question cost me $16,000 after I had paid for everything. However, that one question earned me hundreds of thousands of dollars over the next couple of years. Applying this to my chosen sport, I just knew I needed knowledge I didn't have. So, I reached out. Reaching out to someone who has been there, seen it and done it is a pretty good place to start. I searched out a Mr. Olympia professional online and asked him to coach and mentor me. He agreed, and to quote a cliché, 'the rest is history.'

If you really have a burning desire to be, to do, to have, to achieve something in your life—if it truly is that important to you and you will know if it is—then commit to telling yourself that 'There must be a way.' Then, absolutely commit yourself to finding that way. This one thing, combined with goals and dreams that were vitally important to the very fabric of my being, helped a boy from a council house with a low opinion of himself to become a multi-millionaire, retire at age 38, become a world-level sportsman and a mentor and helper of many others suffering the same challenges I did.

I became the top-level sportsman after all! It only took 30 years! This one belief process took me to the heights I dreamed of and made my dreams a reality.

So, was I living a totally successful and fulfilling life? Did my friends envy me? Did I face any other hardships? Well, it was great until my divorce after eighteen years of marriage and just before lawyers in three countries got involved. Things go downhill when lawyers get involved. At one point in my nightmare, I had a great lady lawyer, who sadly had to take a break for a few months and passed me to a colleague who was a role model for the lawyers people hate. I had to fire that firm, losing whatever I had paid so far and start over again.

So, suffice to say, things are not looking so rosy. Six years of horrific legal battles and a relative who basically absconded with hundreds of thousands of my hard-earned dollars meant that I had to 'start again'. I moved to a new country, worked as a salesperson in the same fragile mental state I had earlier faced. For two years, I shut myself in and worked until I was tired just so that I didn't have to think about how bad things were. I had gone from basically having everything to practically nothing.

My friend Alison was there for me at the end of the phone anytime I needed her. Even when I was raging about the same things, like a broken record time and again, she would patiently support me just by being there. We all have friends when all is well; however, it is the friends who are always there in dark times we must value most. Over time, things got a bit better, and then one day I decided with utter conviction that I was going to get out of this hole.

I decided that I was going to be very wealthy again, and I set myself an enormous figure, which would solve everything. At least it would do so financially. I sat down with utter conviction and belief that 'There must be a way' I can earn that and do that. I had some more learning to do because I was in a new country with new rules and products. Everything was new and unknown. I bit down hard and committed to finding the way. I had procrastinated and wallowed enough. I was basically sick and tired of being sick and tired! I found the way, retired again, and have a great life and freedom and choices.

It's not easy. In fact, many times it's almost impossible to just say and decide 'I'll do that.' For me, anyway, it is. There almost has to be an 'aha' moment that burns deep with an unshakable belief. The reasons have to be as strong as to why that you just 'know' you can and will do it. It doesn't matter that you don't have a clue 'how', you just know that 'There must be a way'. Then you set to the task and work at it until you find the way.

Is it worth it? Absolutely. Can anyone do it? I would like to say yes, but that is up to you. Look at times in your life when you appeared to do the impossible or even really difficult things. What happened before then? Why did you commit, and why was it so important to you? What did you do differently to almost everything else that wasn't so 'spectacular' in your past?

What I have come to believe with every fibre of being is that if you really want it badly enough, then there must be a way. If it really is going to make a life-changing difference and 'it has to happen,' then you will work it out as *there must be a way*. I would like to add that all my personal achievements have been purely an internal challenge. Being number one in a company of 4000 every year was purely a personal challenge. I would ask myself, 'how good could I really be?'

In Asia, I was the top-earning consultant year after year, not to impress anyone else, only to challenge myself to see how good I could really be. Becoming the best sportsman in the world in my chosen sport in a particular year is again an internal challenge for myself.

On a humorous note, I was constantly looking for ways to up my game and fitness levels. Once during my training, I had a deal with a friend of mine Ray. He was SAS. He was 5'5 and 65kg of lean mean spirit. I was 6' and 130kg of gym-driven muscle. I thought I was mentally tough, and so did he. He wanted to improve his gym, and I wanted to have my endurance pushed. So, for two weeks he would train with me in the gym; at weekends, I would go running in the mountains with a weighted pack. What did I learn? My strongest memory is that I learned my lungs work when they are outside of your body. He tortured me up those hills. And I loved it. Then it was my turn. On gym days, I would train an incredibly intense 35 minutes, twice a day. It took him two weeks to last more than 4 minutes in each workout. What did we get from it? An appreciation of focus and hard work and the mental will to find a way to do it and not give up. I always turned up for my mountain 'exercise,' and he always turned up for his two gym 'workouts'.

Once you have found the way, don't quit! Whatever your own motivation is, it doesn't matter. If it is that important to you, an absolute must, then you will find the way. My challenges were driven from an internal frame of reference. I have a friend, let's call him Steve, who has an external frame of reference. He is driven by the spotlight. When someone opens the refrigerator door, Steve jumps into the light and starts combing his hair. It's show time! However, he is number one in his field and wants everyone to know. It drives him. He just 'has to be' and whenever he slips to number two spot he just knows 'There must be a way' to get back to the number one spot. This is when he moves heaven and earth to find it, and he always finds it.

Once a person's goal is set, that 'has to be', the next step is to commit to digging down deep and saying to yourself with total commitment 'There must be a way'. Then, commit to finding it, no matter how long it takes. It'll be worth it!

My biggest achievements that will live with me forever, that I will remember as clear as daylight, and mean the most, were the hardest won. What felt like momentous battles at that time, filled with uncertainty, doubt, and trials, have always meant the most and have given me the greatest pleasure and biggest learning curves in my life. Would I have preferred to have achieved all I have with little or no stress, pain, anguish or frustration, at the time? Absolutely not! If it was easy and everyone could do it, it doesn't mean much. It only has real intrinsic value if it took everything you had, and maybe more, to do it.

Big things take a big effort. Big challenges need bigger solutions. Unknown paths need someone to find the way. If you want to do better, you have to be better; if you want to do more, you have to be more.

One of the greatest things that comes from this is that you'll find the way because 'There must be a way', and then you'll realise 'There must be a way that is your way!'

I f you want to achieve and think it is too hard then Brian's story can help you. Coming from a humble background with little or no success to emulate, Brian became a multimillionaire and world-class athlete, retiring at the age of 38.

His unique style of overcoming the challenges, and of achieving what even he initially thought was impossible, will help you see that almost anything is possible. By learning, watching, and studying as much as possible about what he wanted to achieve and then reinventing the book on how it should be done has made him a world leader, an international coach, and mentor in his chosen field.

Brian has coached and mentored over 5000 sales people, and numerous companies in many countries. The vast majority of them are experiencing their biggest successes in obtaining new clients and enjoying growth in their businesses from working with Brian.

He shares many of his successes through adversity in the hope that this can inspire readers to become men and women of ambition and achievement.

Contact:
Brian Peters
Brianpeters.coach. website
Brianpeterscoaching. FB
Brian Peters LinkedIn

A Personalised Intuitive
Lifestyle Philosophy to
Healthcare

SARAH PATRICK

Have you ever been ill and didn't want to go to the doctor? This may sound strange, but I have experienced the same. It was only while writing this chapter I realised why I didn't want to see a doctor. It was because modern medicine does not come with a personal transformation, and unknowingly, I was desperate for such a transformation.

Today, when I reflect on my life, I am amazed by how its random twists and turns have turned out to be incredibly organised and sequential in nature, giving me all the experiences I needed to reach this point. For example, this moment where I'm writing this chapter is something I have never thought would happen. I was a dyslexic child who had been told "She'll be lucky if she only gets one O-level!" (The British General Certificate of Education Ordinary Level). I never dreamt that I was capable of achieving anything close to what I have, but here I am. After years of fighting the flow of life, I finally learned to trust its innate wisdom.

It all started with me coming into this world. Actually, it was even before that. I have come to recognize that a soul will be persistent in creating events in a life to open doors for transformation, especially if it is what your soul needs and mine most certainly did.

One of the moments when life opened a door to me was just after I had given birth to my third child. At the time, I already had two children, and I thought I could merrily carry on with life without the need to adapt to this life change. However, this wasn't the case and I started to suffer. I felt wired to the mains. My asthma progressively debilitated, and I needed help. It was my wake-up call. I knew if I went to the doctors, I would be prescribed with anti-anxiety medication. I also knew deep down that this wasn't my answer. There was something calling me. So, at the age of thirty-four, I ventured into the unknown territory of complementary medicine. Unknown because I had grown up in a material world and trained to be a biochemist. I had never known there was anything else apart from what I had learnt. When I started raising a family, life handed me an invitation to explore a different way of being. It awakened a sense of purpose, a knowing, and a taking of responsibility on a human level.

In the following decade, with help from and a subsequent education in complementary medicine, I addressed traumas from my childhood, family and soul line. I empowered myself to take responsibility for my health and decided that even though I had been born an asthmatic, I wasn't going to die one.

Another substantial change I made was concerning my family. I took my children out of mainstream education. They weren't labelled 'naughty' or 'genius' and were becoming invisible, turning into numbers in the system. When I took them out of the mainstream, I chose to put them in a Steiner school. It was during my time at this school that I discovered the existence of a thing called the veil, a doorway into another paradigm of existence.

This discovery happened the day when a new friend, whom I had been sharing a lot of time with, spoke about reincarnation during a conversation. I was shocked to my socks by this revelation from her as she was someone whom I had categorised as completely normal. I stood back and reassessed her for signs of madness and couldn't find any. With my scientific hat on, I came to an unwanted conclusion. If everything else about her made sense, then why shouldn't reincarnation make sense, too? I can't say that I liked the conclusion but once the door of possibility opened, the veil opened and my soul began to talk to me.

A few months later she awakened me to my calling. It was to look for 'the roots of modern chronic diseases.' Somewhere deep inside me, I knew I was born with the tools to do it, too. What I couldn't understand then was the purpose behind this. Why had this task been given to me? There were many others out there who had been born seeing through the veil, who seemed totally at ease with this state of being, whilst I was wearing it like an ill-fitting suit and wanted to keep taking it off. The calling made me feel like I was being left on the wrong side of the fence. In my scenario, the height of the fence that I was being asked to scale was immeasurable.

It seemed like I had to move mountains to get there. However, when I really looked, I could see a tiny hole in the fence where a little chink of light was getting through. It was this tiny chink of light that turned this impossible task into an improbable one and increased my determination. While contemplating about this, I understood that everyone else was trying to climb over this unscalable fence too; They, like me, hadn't noticed this little hole at the bottom of the fence where one could squeeze through if one bent down far enough.

The journey to answer my calling, which to find and heal the roots of chronic disease, started in complementary medicine. I didn't understand this field because it made no sense to my scientific training. When I did start my treatment, I observed a shift in my body, and I couldn't ignore that experience. After a few sessions, I was overwhelmed and cried for a week. Years of heavily suppressed events, events that had been suppressed in order for me to survive, came to the surface and I was journeying into my Pandora's box.

What I didn't know about the box was that once opened, it's impossible to close. The only way to stop the plethora of things disturbing me was to empty the contents and get to the bottom. It was while opening the box that I was prompted to ask these questions: "What is the meaning of life?", "What am I supposed to be doing?", "What are we here for?", and "Is there a golden egg?". The only answer I had been given was a rather dreary one from my A-level (British Advanced Level Examination) biology teacher Miss Simpson. She quoted from Darwinian Theory, which asserted that the purpose of life was to reproduce. At thirty-four, this didn't seem a particularly attractive theory. Quite odd really! All this took off precisely because I had another child.

I was looking for something less cold, more inspiring, or more wondrous than the biological drive to procreate. With this 'meaning of life' project in hand, I asked my friends and family, "What do you think the meaning of life is?" I was surprised because they had no answers whatsoever. It seemed like a fundamental question for any human being.

And thus I began my search for an answer. One that would transform me out of this chaotic non-harmonious state of being.

This search was like an addictive beast. It gnawed and it consumed without a care. It wouldn't leave me alone. It hooked me in. I remember thinking how I would happily hand out advice to anyone thinking of opening Pandora's box. I will tell them not to do it and if possible, to remain in ignorant bliss. I went to talks and noticed how they, too, were consumed by the search. "We're nearly there", they would say, and it always seemed to be nearly there. It picked us up into a feverish pitch, only to throw us back into the pit of disappointment, giving us another task to conquer. It was like participating in a Greek myth *The 12 labours of Hercules* or *Sisyphus*, the King who had to roll a stone up a hill only to find that when he fell asleep, the stone would roll back down the hill. My answers and solutions seemed just as amazing as theirs. It was as tangible and as believable.

I consumed endless enlightenment books searching for a way out. I was told I was supposed to be enjoying myself, to bathe in the light, to let go, and to accept all that came up from the dark. It wasn't pleasant. There was only one book that alluded to this journey to meet the soul as not being one for the fainthearted.

When I was in the deepest part of my journey, I sought refuge from a friend, who was a kinesiologist. After a series of muscle testing, she announced that I needed to eat chocolate. I was relieved that I wasn't being asked to go deeper. We dived into her well-stocked larder and consumed chocolate and felt so much better afterwards.

Later, my confidence grew and I tackled the things my journey threw at me. More importantly, I began to take them in my stride. But I did get bored of the seemingly long time it took to get to some sort of finishing post. There were many moments when I announced to my family we could go out for a pizza to celebrate my finding of the answer. Sadly, as I would find out the next day, the unrest had settled back in again. Patience was the answer. I began to learn. I remember hearing someone recall the expression "In God's Time," and I started to take this to heart. I reflected how there didn't seem to be anything I could do to get the answer faster than the way I was currently doing. There was no accelerator provided with which I could push my foot to the floor. I realized the timing of finding my answer was out of my control. I had been under the belief that getting worked up and stressed about it would magically create a time shift and bring the answer closer.

Slowly, as I plodded through this amazing, frustrating, addictive and continually disappointing journey, I finally reached a point where I felt normal. However, this wasn't exactly what I was looking for. At the start of this journey, I had decided that I wasn't looking for the OM or asking to sit cross-legged for Utopia. I knew I wanted to be able to enjoy the beauty that already exists around us and to enjoy the opportunities that meet us. There is so much in life that I didn't need anything else.

Finding normal, however, did stop me in my tracks. My first thought was "How does one sell normal?" I'd been expecting something a little more profound. I could imagine myself on a street corner with a placard in my hand proclaiming "Let me tell you the secrets to being normal", whilst all other gurus were selling sunshine, heaven, and permanent bliss. However, life had taught me to be careful of bliss and heaven. The last time I'd been in heaven was after I had come around from a general anaesthetic for removing my appendix. The nurse was shaking me "Wake up Sarah, wake up!" I, believing I was in heaven, did some quick mental arithmetic to deduce that the only way to stay in heaven was to die. So, I announced to my nurse in my opiated state "I want to die, I want to die." My nurse replied, "I don't think you do, Sarah." Then, of course, she dragged me back into reality. In the state I was in, I sent logical profound text messages to my friends, which I was too embarrassed to read later in the light of day. It's amazing how something can feel so logical one moment and not very logical afterwards. Later, when I was talking to a friend who works with street users, she said "Now you can see why people get addicted to heroin." That was a sobering thought. Perhaps normal is safer. If such highs come during the lows, perhaps this journey is all a symptom of addiction.

There is some lovely work by Gabor Maté. He talks about addictions being set up in our early childhood and further discusses how we don't actually have to experience traumatic events to create them. A sensitive nature or a momentary insecure blip is all that is required to create an addiction. Addiction doesn't have to mean drugs and medication; it can look like sugar or toast and comfort eating or perfectionism. The keyword here is a drive. It makes us do something and later goes out of control without our knowledge. All these addictions are the same; we are looking for those substances or behavioural traits to get something that we are not getting in our lives. They are a way of self-medicating. As we repair and find fulfilment, the less we are reliant on our addictive tendencies. As one goes up, the other goes down.

Sorry, I'm digressing a bit here. Let's go back to finding being normal. It's probably at this point I can hear you think "This isn't what I'm looking for because I'm unique. I don't want to think of myself as normal. I want to be extraordinary. I have dreams, and I have things to do!" Believe me, I had the same convictions, too!

But hang on a moment

Now, how about when you go to the doctor because you have some pain or a slight niggle in your body? The doctor examines you and takes some blood samples. At this point, everyone hopes to be normal, don't they? So how does that work? The need for us to be normal and extraordinary at the same time. Is there a paradigm that exists for this?

Like many other people, I, too, have a list of unpleasant things that have happened to me. Even if you haven't experienced all these things personally, you're here probably because you have a sensitive nature or because the effect of what you experienced was powerful enough to affect you permanently. What actually happened is irrelevant. What is much more important is how it has affected you.

When I delved into my soul history, I realised that it is at least as old as the planet. This makes it impossible for us, on the soul level, to not have acquired a lengthy list of bad things that happened to us. It's also impossible for us to have always been the victim, which means that we must have been the perpetrator at some point. Now, that's not a nice thought. If I were to look at my list and yours, it would read something like this: 301 stabbings, 142 drownings, 318 murders, 3 burnt at the stake, 22 died in childbirth, 15 rapes, 23 poisonings, and so on. It seemed to me that if I took each event on the list one by one, it would take at least a lifetime or longer to heal my soul. But what of this life? Wasn't this life supposed to be about living it? Did I really want to spend all my life going through all these events in my soul journey one by one? Not at all. So, I decided to put the whole lot in a bag and call it a 'mess!'

What I learned is:

- Deeply embedded illnesses have a spiritual, physical, and mental connection. In my case, my crisis had been a disguised message from the soul asking me to find a natural solution to my asthma.
- Possessing physical, mental, and spiritual health is the backbone of allowing change to happen at the deepest level.

It was during this journey that I saw myself as a part of the collective consciousness. At the same time, my children were making the transition from the sanctuary of the family home into the big wide world and my client base was growing. It was these things that made me take a bigger interest in what was happening in the world around us.

The Modern World

Today, humanity is in a period of reflection. There is a change in the air. It is a moment when humanity is being offered an opportunity to come out of denial, caused mainly by the suffering and trauma of two world wars. It is a time to listen to what our bodies are telling us, to have confidence in our innate wisdom, and to trust ourselves again.

It's very difficult to reach one's potential if we are in poor health. There are always exceptions to the rule—that is one of the beauties of human nature. There is no one solution that fits all. The constitutions in the western world are getting weaker with each passing generation. Ever since 1945, there has been an increase in the faith that medicines will deliver the answer to diseases. I have seen this accompanied by an increase in fear around personal health as people cling to medication as though it is life itself. People have lost touch with their innate wisdom. We all have moments in our life where biomedical procedures and treatments have saved our lives. Looking back, I can trace seven such procedures. I wouldn't have survived if it hadn't been for modern medicine. But modern medicine is a short-term solution to illness, not a permanent one. Luckily here in the UK, there are medical doctors on the television like Dr. Rangan Chatterjee and Dr. Chris van Tulleken who are educating the public on how all medicines come with side effects and are teaching us to look at reducing our dependency on them, along with encouraging us to investigate alternative ways to achieve good health. They are joined by celebrity chefs like Jamie Oliver and Hugh Fearnley-Whittingstall who actively campaign for improved diets and food sources.

In developing countries, where the environment is harsher and access to medical care is limited, it is a requirement to have a strong constitution to survive. Energetic workers have noticed how these people respond extraordinarily fast to metaphysical medicine. They love working in these countries. Their results are so much faster and magical. Here in the West, we are like old cars, run down with acid batteries and crank handles that need turning to get us moving. It takes so much more effort for us to get going and continue running.

In our Western society, there is an epidemic of chronic disease. Let's look at some of the statistics.

- One in four people in 2018 will have a mental problem (BBC1, The Doctor Who Gave up Drugs).
- The NHS (National Health Service, a publicly funded healthcare system in the UK) prescribed a record number of depressants in 2016 and the number of pills prescribed to patients has more than double over the last decade. (Guardian, a British newspaper, June 17).
- NHS figures showed one in eleven adults are being prescribed potentially addictive drugs. These drugs have doubled in the last 15 years (Telegraph, a British newspaper, Feb 2018).
- The Health Survey for England 2016 showed that in 2016 only 26% of adults ate five or more portions of fruit and vegetables a day.

There is something going on at a deeper level that is leading people to become more dissatisfied with the way they are living their life. With the development of the modern world and the addition of new chemicals and new ways of living, these factors are placing an unprecedented demand on the status of our health. In any case, we need to probe deeper and be more creative and more intuitive at solving the problems each new generation is bringing. As biomedicine becomes more advanced, we can survive in weaker constitutional states. My journey as a biochemist and psychic is to explore and learn how we can return our constitutional strength to its full potential, so we can live our lives to the full and help our next generation.

I think we all want to be healthy, and I genuinely believe this. I think the reason we are not making healthy choices is because of the underlying issues that prevent us. Health matters to all of us and getting healthy can be easy or very difficult. When we have good health on our physical, mental and spiritual levels, we attain the ability to freely express our inner power and harness our true energy.

This power arises when our vibrational inner presence, words, and actions are aligned with our truth and the world around us.

When the physiological values in us are normal, the body becomes less stressed. A peaceful state transcends over the body, freeing us up to use our inner power and potential. I remember when I questioned chronically ill people what they would do when they were well again. Their most common response was that they wished to go on a holiday. I was surprised by this answer until I realised what an enormous amount of energy being chronically ill uses up. How much energy it simply takes them to hold their body together, to employ coping strategies, and at the same time search for and question new solutions.

If your physiological values are not normal, the body will attempt to drive them back into homeostasis. When this can't be done, the body sends a message that things aren't quite right and something needs to be done. It's at this point that the body goes into a survival response.

It seems perfectly logical to employ our minds to search for the solution. What we haven't recognized is that our thinking, too, is in a survival response. In this mode there are no new thought or new solutions; it's a rerun of all the thoughts we have had before. For new thoughts or the ability to see a new way through, the mind needs to be in a reflective state. When we go into this state, we notice it is an expansive state: a state that allows peripheral factors and our inner wisdom to shine through. For example, we all recognise the increase in eureka moments that happen when we are in the shower, driving the car, or walking in nature.

What About the Outside Environment?

In the book *Chasing the Scream: The Opposite of Addiction is Connection*, Johann Hari writes there are two primary areas of life that cause driven behaviour. The first is childhood trauma, and the second is a person's living environment. If you grow a plant in the wrong soil, it struggles to grow well. People are the same. When I became a mother with young children, I lived in a small village in the countryside; it was an idyllic place to bring up children. We experimented with nature, incubated chickens, planted vegetables, put up tents, and played badminton in the garden. Once the children grew up, I became depressed. The large garden became a millstone around my neck. Almost every weekend was taken up mowing the lawn, keeping the garden tidy, and pruning the hedges; everyone loved the look of it, but no one ever went into it. They just looked and admired. I concluded that I might as well have a projected image of a garden on the window to achieve the same result.

What I hadn't realised was the garden had been a tool, which I had used to bring up my children as a contentious and dedicated parent. This was extraordinarily important to me, but the large garden wasn't something that was a part of my needs as an individual. Once the children left, the garden became something I was hoarding. I didn't need it anymore. It was only through life coaching I realised I had made an unconscious contract to my children to keep the family home until they could fly away from the family nest. Unconscious contracts are very powerful things. They can make us miserable if we aren't aware of them. Once the children left home and the unconscious contract was completed, I felt free to accept offers. When I moved to London, the remainder of my comfort eating, which I had been using to self-medicate my emotions, fell away.

When I look back at my life, I see how every event has brought me to this moment. I see how these events have been pre-arranged. However, the way in which I respond to these events isn't prearranged. It's as though I am being given an opportunity to change the way I respond. As I change the way I respond, it changes a resonance that ripples back, back through my family line, back through my soul line, and back through humanity. This ripple effect is much more extensive than the 'doing something' effect. We can affect so many more people through our metaphysical connections. The science writer Guy Murchie believes that no two people anywhere on the earth can be more distantly related than 50th cousins. So, it doesn't matter if you are out there changing the world in a big way or growing tomatoes in a small village, your contribution to the whole can be the same.

Experience has taught me that there are wider elements at work (including my unconscious self) that are working together to return me to my natural balanced state. It often happens that my conscious self is the last to know of my plans. I have learned to trust there is an answer, even if the answer may not be for the question I asked. It has allowed me to become happier with not knowing. I have found that life's plans for me are much grander and more complex than the plans I had made for myself. If you give up the need to control how your whole life unfolds and instead learn to put your trust in life, it is amazing to see the path it takes. When I am in my groove and make choices that bring all parts of my whole being together, life flows. That doesn't mean there aren't any hiccups, but they do resolve and I am continually surprised by how they do.

During a "3 Principles" course, I saw emotions were just like the weather. They come and go. However, during our lifetime, especially during childhood when the survival instinct is at its peak, we adapt by neurologically rewiring ourselves to think certain emotions are more important than others. When we prioritise an emotion or feeling above others, it indicates that we may have a belief that isn't serving us. Rather than buying into that emotion and overthinking it, we need to step back into a space of reflection and let the answer come to us rather than us going to the answer. I have a saying that goes "I have fear, but I am not frightened of it." Emotions are like a palette of colours; together they represent the completeness of the human experience, and without one, you couldn't appreciate another. When I mentioned this to a friend, she told me that she'd heard that it was part of the soul's journey to experience and digest them all.

I would never have got to where I am today—the journey to becoming a whole human being—if it hadn't been for the other people who turned up in my life to help. In my searching period, a group of ten people just appeared and volunteered to help, to be my guinea pigs, to cherish my soul, and to believe in me. I was extraordinarily lucky because it helped me see the archetypal patterns of humanity and supported me when the going got tough.

I have seen what I give out in life is reflected in what it gives me back; the more whole I become, the faster this return of serve happens. When I do give out rubbish, it is usually because there is a hidden emotion behind it. I love the moment when I recognise the emotion as it arises out of the fog of generalized anxiety. It gives me something to work with, but this doesn't always happen. Tim Ferris has a created a tool to help him move through difficult transitions in his life. He takes 30 minutes to face the problem head-on. His tactic is to question the fear and turn it from being something irrational into something rational. He starts by drawing three columns. In the first column, he writes down everything he is specifically frightened of and this has to be specific rather than a vague emotion. In the second column, he writes down all the steps he can take to avoid the things in the first column from happening. In the final column, he writes down what he could do to repair the situation if it did happen. I took an alternative approach, a 10-ish step technique when I moved out of the family home. I did one small step at a time; when I did that small step, I choose to pretend this step wasn't part of a much bigger overwhelming transition in my life.

I used to procrastinate relentlessly until I realized putting off something wasn't going to change my emotional reaction to it. As for the other tactic of waiting until I felt like it, well, I could be waiting forever. My trick to getting an undesired task done is to not think about it and when I do, to get in quick and start before my emotions overpower me. The more I do this, the easier it becomes; it is as though the emotions learn that there is no point in bothering me. Whilst writing this chapter—a huge deal for a dyslexic—I outwitted my emotions by getting up at 6.00 am and sitting at a table and writing, with nothing in between the getting up and writing. Most tasks are more about ticking the box than about achieving perfection. I have learned now what most of my strengths and weaknesses are. Having weaknesses is part of being human . They provide me with an opportunity to connect with others and share our strengths and weaknesses.

I'm a great admirer of the phrase that we "Stand on the shoulders of giants." This acknowledges if someone has done something before, it's our human inevitability and in our genes to be able to improve on it. Think of a freshly ploughed field without a clear path to the gate. Everyone is lost as to how to get from one side of the field to the other. But once somebody leaves a track to the gate, the next person sees this track as a whole path and magically and delightfully improves on it.

My story is one where I started off in the wrong place and how I found my way to the right place. The journey took me to a space where quantum physics meets material sciences, bringing together both my skills and experience of being a scientist and a psychic. I've worked as a remedy maker since 2002, making bespoke metaphysical cognitive remedies for people with chronic disease. The experience has taught me there are three levels where chronic disease can reside and how to go about healing them.

The Three Levels of Chronic Disease

Level 1: Changes to lifestyle

- <u>Cleaning up our diet</u>: Adding in more fruits and vegetables, doing the 5-a-day, decreasing processed foods, drinking 1½ litres of water every day, and removing comfort substances like sugar, alcohol, nicotine, coffee and tea from our diet can work wonders. If you have chronic disease residing in level 2 or 3, removing substances or making behavioural changes that you rely on for self-medication may make this impossible.
- <u>Sleep</u>: This is vital to our wellbeing as a good night's sleep heals our body and thoughts.
- <u>Meditation or taking time out to walk daily in nature</u>: There are some great meditation apps available now or you could read the book *Bliss More* by Light Watkins. Start short with 10mins. This is the key to success. There are also some good gratitude journaling apps. It is about finding what works for you.
- <u>Having family and friends and a good personal social life</u>: Humans are social animals. Most people, when they are given the space to reflect, wish they had spent more time with friends and family.
- <u>Self-expression</u>: Who are we outside work? What are our hobbies? This is so important to being well in ourselves. Do something that expresses yourself. Remember the child who comes home from school and shows you their drawing with that wondrous delight on their face? It is about the freedom to express, never about how good it is. Hobbies can include drawing, painting writing, playing an instrument, dancing,

cooking, sewing, woodwork or just about anything that takes you into creative play.

- Exercise: With our increasingly modern lifestyles, it is important for to pay attention to our bodies and avoid being at risk from chronic disease. The main factor to succeed in the long run is to ensure that exercise contains an element of fun. It should be wholeheartedly enjoyed. For most people, the addition of a social element is the key to long-term success.

Level 2: For stubborn conditions that won't complete their healing process by implementing the above.

- Employ a metaphysical energy expert, be it a transformational coach, a homeopath, a Reiki healer, an acupuncturist, a cranial-sacral therapist, a reflexologist or someone of your choice. Select a method or practitioner you have a connection with or a methodology that appeals to you personally.

Level 3: For people whose core condition does not budge but may experience peripheral improvements with any of the above methods.

- This level mainly includes people who have had a chronic condition for a large proportion of their lives and have tried everything. To explain this statement, it is useful to use a metaphor of the broken plate. Imagine you are angry with your mother and you throw a plate against the wall and it breaks. It doesn't matter how many anger management courses you go through, the plate isn't going to be fixed because it is fundamentally broken. What it needs is glue, which will stick it back together again. This has nothing to do with the breaking of the plate and thus requires lateral thinking.

Good health is the key to making successful transformations and transitions in life. Good health makes it easy to live a fulfilling life.

So, what is the meaning of life? Why are we here? For me, it's simply being free to get on with living and enjoying the amazing beauty that surrounds us on this planet.

S arah Patrick is a scientist and psychic who had a calling to find and heal the roots of chronic disease. She believes that good spiritual, mental, and physical health is fundamental for achieving the transformations necessary for a free and fulfilling life.

Sarah Patrick is a Remedy Maker and Transformational Coach.

Please contact Sarah at: www.phareremedy.co.uk or via Linkedin: Sarah Patrick "Time to Begin"

How the Most Challenging Relationship of Our Life Sets Us on the Path to Extraordinariness

DEEPTI G GUJAR

It is 7 in the morning, and there is a rhythmic clang of vessels coming from the kitchen. There is a quietness in her footsteps. I hear her speak even through the thickest of my sleep. I hear all the stories that she has received on one of her WhatsApp groups, her political opinions, and her admiration of God as if he were a real person. I wake up much later and ask her for tea. Even though my friends rave about my tea or *chai*-making skills, her tea is nirvana. Sleepy-eyed, I drag myself to a bath and by the time I come out, the air is perfumed with fresh lemongrass and *chai*. This is the fragrance of home.

She is already at the counter with one foot propped up on her other knee, rolling out *rotis*. It's half of a *vrikshasana*, or the tree pose in yoga. She is in yoga. She is one with me and I with her. It has taken me more than three decades to get here. To flow into this oneness. To be in union with her.

Childhood

I was around 5 when I first became aware of her existence. Because I was a C-section baby, I literally felt cut off from my life force ever since I was born. I felt cut off from her, and I had no idea who she was in my universe. There was always this sense of …emptiness. I felt that I was missing some part of me, but how could I elucidate that when I was just 5?

It was around then that we moved into a new house. We finally had a bathroom in this one, and I remember her being very happy about it. For the inauguration, we were supposed to have a traditional ritual and she insisted that I put my foot first in the house as a symbol of prosperity. She believed that I was a personification of the goddess of prosperity, or *Lakshmi*. It was all supposed to be a big deal; for me, it was simply about following instructions. At that time, my consciousness was only composed of feelings and images; I didn't have any of my own thoughts. I was, therefore, a quiet and obedient child.

Since my parents were working, I had to come back to an empty flat after school; as a result, I was put up in a crèche until I was 7. Since my father's shift started very early in the morning, she would take me to the crèche at around 10 am each day with bags full of food as well as her belongings. I remember her carrying me along with all these bags. They were heavy and weighed her down; she was hardly 5 feet tall. She also had a severe migraine that was triggered by the light of the morning sun. It was so severe that if she ever accidentally watched the sun rise, she would be throwing up and would have a massive headache all day and had to be drugged into sleep. I remember waking up during those days and feeling like she was lost to the void, beyond any of our reach. On those days, my dad would take over and make sure that I was fed.

By the time I was seven, I was acutely aware of how she struggled each day to drop me off at the crèche every morning, walking through the sunlight. I was especially aware of the brutality of it during my summer holidays, when her migraines occurred weekly. I was overwhelmingly aware that it was her will to take care of me that made her go to these extreme lengths. One day I told her that I want to start staying home on my own; instead of a crèche, I wanted to come back home.

After triple-checking with me to make sure that this is what I truly wanted, she took out a copy of the house keys and stitched them into my school bag with a long string so I wouldn't lose them; she told me that I had to stay safe. I had to make sure that no one was following me as I walked home from where my auto rickshaw, the one that picked me up from my school, dropped me. I was to do the same as I climbed three floors to our apartment. I gave her my word that I would stay safe. Around this time, I had made some friends in the 5-storeyed apartment building that housed roughly 4 families on each floor. They were all very nice to me, and I trusted them.

One day, one of my neighbours' son who was around 18 at the time called me over to play. He gave me some chocolate to eat, and started playing a game of touch. He told me it was our own secret game, and that I shouldn't tell anyone about it. This 'game' started with him undressing me. Over the next summer months, this 'game' went much further along, and my summer days were all spent playing this very engaging game. It took me out of the loneliness that had started creeping up on me because I stayed alone at home for 4–5 hours every day before either parent returned. This game continued even when school started. By then, it had become a fancy game of hide and seek. We were hiding from our parents. He pretended, on occasion, to be my boyfriend and even wrote me love notes. It was all very new and fascinating to me. This went on, surprisingly, for about 2 to 3 years. It had become a pleasure-addiction for me and a good way to avoid loneliness.

One day, he asked me to convince another friend of mine to join our 'secret game.' Enthusiastically, I got her there, but the moment he started undressing her, she started crying. She was around a year younger than me. In order to quieten her, he sent her back. I didn't think much of it until that evening when her mother knocked on our door and asked to speak to my mother. She said that I had upset her daughter. I went along, not knowing what I had done. It was then that her mother talked about her daughter getting undressed and how shameful it was that I had dragged her into something like that.

Inadvertently, I was blamed. My mother immediately reprimanded me and told me that what I had done was awful. It was that evening when I first felt a gush of blood raging through my heart all the way down to my feet. It was a set of sensations that I later came to understand as shame mixed with anger. The next few weeks became the most painful and vivid moments of my life. After I put together all the information that came my way from my friend's mother, it hit me that what was happening to me was not play. It was abuse. I was being fooled, and I had been betrayed.

I tried to 'break it off' with my neighbour, but he had become violent by then. He had started threatening me. It was becoming horrific to come back home each day and find him waiting for me. I lived in terrifying fear. I ran past him each day and locked my door. The house felt like a prison until my mother returned home each evening. My own thoughts had begun to attack me. I was all of 9, but I felt older than that. I never let my mother know about any of this. She only found out when he started slipping notes through the small letter opening in the door. That evening was a nightmare. She asked me what was going on. Why are there these love notes? She was outraged. She knew instinctively that something wrong had been happening and she tried to question me, but I was sobbing inconsolably. She questioned that guy, and he got away by apologising. He said he was just playing a prank to scare me and that he wouldn't do it again. I didn't have the will to tell her what had happened because of how ashamed I was of betraying her trust. I had let her down, and I had broken my promise. That evening was a defining point in our relationship, one that impacted me deeply.

I was outraged at myself in ways that I only understood decades later when I went into therapy. That day, I had shut her off forever because I didn't deserve her love. As I stood there sobbing, not letting a single word out, I felt like Munch's painting *Scream*. I was screaming inside, but I had no voice. Strangely, I also felt very let down by her. Why had she not punished me for what had happened? Why hadn't she probed more? Why didn't she understand without me having to explain anything to her?

I made up several stories in my head. The bitterest one, and the one that would become the toughest to undo in my later years, was that she didn't care. So, I shut myself from her. I went cold. I was about 9 and suddenly felt like dying to escape all the pain, rage, and shame colliding within me all the time. Unable to bear the onslaught of emotions, raging thoughts, and the sensations that these produced in my body, I went numb. I lived like a zombie. I would function, but I wasn't able to feel. I couldn't process what had happened. I couldn't feel my way back into my reality and my world. Whatever little spark of connection I had had with her, it had gone out.

Entering the Tunnel

I was violently thrust into rage as I hit my teens and found myself coming out of the spell of daze. From an obedient, reticent child, I had become a teen with mercurial spells of extreme rage. I would bang the doors of my house, hurl abuses at her at the top of my voice, and make sure that I did everything that was the exact opposite of what she had asked me to do. All that numbness had fermented into a deep hatred for her.

Those years were excruciatingly painful for both of us. Parallelly, life had been taking a toll on her. She had already gone through one spell of depression during which I saw her being carried by my father and my uncle to a psychiatrist every night. It had lasted for a few months and then she was out, but it had changed her. She had become frightfully angry as a person. I would trigger anger in her at the slightest provocation. Just as I blamed her for all my life's agony, I had become her punching bag. At one point, we would hurl dishes and heavy cookware at each other in our battles, just to show the other who was angrier. My hatred for her grew. We barely spoke to each other in those brief moments of ominous calm between the storms. The house was a battlefield.

My father, a very sensitive musician, was constantly breaking down while trying to establish peace between us. We weren't a family.

This rage didn't leave me even as I went through my teens into my twenties and began pursuing engineering. Even that was a choice made in defiance. My mother wanted me to pursue commerce, and she violently disagreed with my choice of pursuing arts. As a 'compromise', I chose to study engineering so that she wouldn't get her way. It, therefore, came as a big surprise for us both when I started getting very high grades. For the first time in my life, I was receiving attention for the right reasons and it made her proud. Because of that, I started remembering those years before the sexual abuse when there used to be a tangible connection between us. No sooner had I started to remember some deeply buried memories, she hit another kind of 'depression' again.

This time it was much worse. She was in an altered state of violent paranoia interspersed with very clear episodes of consciousness, where she knew what was happening to her and would become frightened like a little child. Every day, at around 4.30 am, she would wake up screaming. She felt that someone was beating her up and choking her. Sometimes she showed us marks on her body to prove that someone was doing this to her. My dad would often break down in these mornings and come to me helpless and in tears.

One of those mornings, I held her hand as she was crying. Her eyes were wide and bewildered, and her mind was in a state of acute emotional pain that I could not connect to. I tried to reach out to her through that state and tell her that I loved her, but couldn't. I instantly felt that it was a lie. I couldn't look into her eyes and tell her I loved her when almost every minute of my day I would be talking to myself of how much I hated her. I didn't want her to die, but I was ashamed of my reason. I wanted her to live just so that she would look after and cook for my younger brother and me. This piercing introspection rattled the foundations of who I thought I was. All the hate that I had accumulated against her turned against me. That evening, she took my younger brother and me to the terrace on the roof of the building to commit suicide. It all seemed like a daze, and I still don't know what held her back. But she came back. I numbed out again.

It was my final year of engineering, and I was losing my grades because of the inner battle I was going through. I had lost my sense of what was real. I had questions that would no longer let me sleep peacefully. I had lost trust in who I was and in life itself. Every morning, I would wake up with the terror that I would find her gone. I associated waking up early with this fear, so I became a late riser. In my eyes, I had failed in the worst possible way. I could not tell her that I loved her. That was a big failure for me. I was afraid that she was going to die with only violent memories of us fighting, remembering a thankless child whom she had raised with all that she had. It was the most painful recurring thought at the time. What added to this was the inner confusion: I didn't know if I really loved her or if I was really just an entitled child trying not to lose her mother for her own selfish gains. This confusion haunted me night and day.

It was no surprise that I lost my grades and went downhill emotionally. I hit another episode of numbness. I didn't care about my life. I got enough grades to get into an engineering college of my choice. In the meantime, she began recovering. But not through psychiatry, through something known as 'faith healing'. I felt emotionally disconnected from her because we didn't have much of a relationship left. Even after she began recovering, we had severe rage clashes.

A Light Appears at the End of the Tunnel

After completing my bachelor's, I was recruited into one of the top IT organisations in the world. My joining process was bittersweet because I was going through my first real breakup, and it ended violently. Inevitably, my mother had a major role to play in that breakup, and I blamed her for taking away what I thought was 'my one true love.' Soon after the breakup, I found *Many Lives, Many Masters* by Dr Brian Weiss being sold on the footpath of a popular shopping street in my hometown. I began reading that book after dinner, around midnight, and did not put it down until it was finished, around 2 am, with tears rolling down my face. I had finally found a place that would get me the answers to my questions. In those days, we had *Orkut*, a social platform that preceded Facebook. It had forums or groups that one could join based on one's interest. I immediately looked for one based on past life regression, the topic on which the book was based, and sent a question to see if there was somebody who worked on past life regression in India. Within 3 months, I was attending the workshop of a past life regression teacher, who Dr Brian Weiss himself recommended. He went on to become my first and my most influential spiritual and life teacher, mentor, and guide.

I spent my weekdays on software programming, and my weekends on reading more of Dr Brian Weiss. My first past life regression experience utterly convinced that I had come to the right source. Dots about my life started connecting in ways that started to make me come alive again. It helped me find the completion I had craved for. After the workshop, my anger towards my mother lessened for a while. It was like a tsunami that had abated.

I asked her to come along with me to this spiritual teacher's office for a one-on-one session, and it touched me deeply that she was open to it. For 3 days, we went into separate rooms and were taken 'under' to experience our past lives. I was eager to understand why I experienced abuse as a child. After I came out of a particularly horrific past life memory, my teacher asked me if my mother knew about the trauma. When I shook my head, he asked me if I was ready to change that and would be ready to include my mother in my trauma.

I was very resistant to this idea, so I gave him excuses. I said that she wouldn't understand, but I was mostly afraid that she would feel let down by me. I sheepishly admitted that. He smiled and asked me to trust her instead of being so sure of the outcome. That evening, in the presence of my teacher and his wife, I finally shared the experiences that I could recall with her. She was shocked, but her only response was that "It happens to a lot of women."

I felt crushed by her cavalier response; I had wanted her to say that she was sorry. I didn't get that apology, so I felt embarrassed and pushed aside this incident. Situations unfolded in such a way that I had to leave for Switzerland almost immediately after these sessions, and everyone was caught up in this excitement. It was a big deal for someone with just 9 months of career experience to be sent at the client's end, which in this case was a very demanding and high profile Swiss bank. When I reached Switzerland, I felt that deep and primal consciousness within me relax in that beautiful, restful calmness. For the first time in my life, I felt at home. I was terrified of walking on the streets in India, but in Zurich, I walked the streets at night. I met a handsome Indian man and fell in love with him because his *chai* was just as special as my mother's. I started to miss her viscerally.

In six months, it was winter and S.A.D was affecting me heavily. I would wake up, call her, and cry on the phone like a baby. I wanted to go back to her. I would apologise for the hell that I had put her through. I wrote her letters in my diary that I never sent. It was almost as if I had begun grieving, but I had no idea what I was grieving. I was barely 21. When I was sent back from Switzerland, due to their predictions of the oncoming financial recession, I had mixed emotions. I wanted to get married to the man that I had met in Switzerland, but I understood that our relationship would not survive the distance. On the other hand, Switzerland felt like a home to me. It was what an ideal home is supposed to be: calm, tranquil, and safe. To someone like me, who associated 'home' with constant trauma and upheavals, Switzerland felt like the proverbial heaven. It was a tranquil womb where nothing could go wrong. When I finally had to go back, I felt like I was being snatched away from my source, my belonging. The only good thing about moving back to India was that I would finally get to meet my mother again.

Beginnings of Transformation

After resuming my job in India, I felt extremely displaced. I didn't feel any sense of belonging in India. All my friends who started their careers with me had either left their jobs or had been placed abroad for work. The only thing that I found worth continuing was past life therapy. So, I sought out my spiritual teacher again and decided to pursue an even more intense past life therapy training course.

That course was the first in a series of intense, life-altering transformations. As part of it, we went through fourteen hours of regression each day for six days, trying various ways of going into altered states of consciousness through techniques such as hypnosis. I relived past lives with my mother and travelled to the ugliest of memories that carried the seeds of the hatred that I felt for her. *"Reliving is releasing"* was our mantra during the workshop. A lot of my relationships simply unravelled, and the intense rage within me was replaced with an intense connectedness to everything around me. By the end of the workshop, I was living through an altered state where my feet simply didn't 'touch the ground.' I felt like I was floating. I was supernaturally high, and I began experiencing moments of unconditional and unabated love for my mother that did not carry even the desire for expression. I learnt to exist around her. It felt like an extraordinary gift. I could see my relationship with her as the sum of all our lifetimes together. It helped me understand *karma* in the truest sense. It was extraordinary balance.

I was still riding this spiritual high when I decided to go for another workshop that my spiritual teacher had organised 'to heal our inner child,' a term coined by Carl Jung. Little did I know that my entire existence was about to be uprooted. In this six-day intensive workshop, I was spiralling down into severe mood swings and altered states that I had only experienced as a child. I spontaneously started reliving the long silences that were part of my childhood when I could not construct full sentences. I often 'forget' that I was 23 and acted like a 7 year-old during the workshop. The exercises we were taken through in the workshop brought up all the pain and memories that had been suppressed so rapidly that it drowned my identity and my sense of normalcy. It opened vivid memories of abuse that I had forgotten. What was worse was that the 'processing' of these memories was not complete when I returned home at the end of that workshop. What ensued was a bitter fight with my mother. In the spur of the moment, I packed my bags and ran away from home with the help of a friend who was accompanying me. I had even threatened to call the cops on her. It was a shock to our whole family. Such was the intensity of my emotional pain that I soon came down with a fever as I reached the city where my spiritual teacher who had conducted the workshop lived.

When he found out what had transpired, he and his team immediately took me under their wing and set up a place for me to stay in their office. Over the next few months, he worked tirelessly with me to release every memory and every belief of my life that was giving rise to my destructive emotions. He began taking me through the basics of spirituality while showing me how my beliefs had shaped my reality. I stayed in a room all day in states that altered between childhood memories that brought up intense grief and past life memories that defied all sense of reality.

This entire phase was like unearthing every brick out of an ancient foundation. It was a painful and slow but a much-needed rebirth. I started gaining a new sense of identity. A new version of normalcy started returning. I started connecting and relating to my feelings in a new way; towards the end of that stay, he told me something that changed the course of my life. He asked me to go back to my mother. He asked me to take that relationship to the level of unconditional love. You must learn to see her as your greatest spiritual force and teacher, he said. That, would be 'living enlightenment.' The day that she completely stopped being a trigger for me would be the day I would truly be free. I wondered if a day would ever come where we could exist without a struggle between us. It felt like a distant dream.

And so back I went, packing my bags again, to find my way back home with this single-minded quest.

The Long Road Home

Back at home, there was no home. 'We' were in a state of absolute dysfunction as a family. My mother refused to talk and refused to forgive me despite taking me back in. I was jobless, penniless, and dependant on her. This was against her values in life. She expected me to be entirely independent and strong, but the opening of my innate sensitivity made me feel raw and vulnerable since my return. She thought that I had joined a cult, a cult that had given me violent values, and that was the reason that I fought with her. She refused to let me connect with my spiritual teacher because of this. I had no idea how to even begin the repairs. My only source of light was a friend who I had briefly connected with in my inner child workshop. While I had much to face and overcome, this friend had just experienced deep completions in her own journey as a mother. I started visiting her, asking her questions, venting my frustrations, and breaking down as my mother hurled verbal abuses back at home for having betrayed her and violated her trust. This friend started teaching me the basic technique of witnessing, through watching my breath, and told me to go back home and practice that. I wanted to escape, but she, like my spiritual teacher, pointed out my flight response to emotional pain and asked me to step right into the heart of it, rather than escaping or fighting it. I had to work my way towards this long road to freedom.

I had become so good at fighting and answering at my mother that it had become an automatic response. She asked me to drop the battle and allow my mother's pain to penetrate me. This friend, who I now call my spiritual mentor, became something beyond that for me in that phase. She became my first and only *guru*. I would often see her practicing these very same things with her mother; seeing her do that became the force that gave me the humility and the will to make this journey with my own mother. As soon as my mother woke up, she would hurl verbal abuses at me. Inevitably, I would wake up listening to these with tears of suffering. Following my *guru*'s words, I started forcing myself out of that urge, the urge to lie down like a wounded animal and be a victim and instead examine the pain. I learnt to witness it and breathe into the sensations it triggered in my body in response. My mother would rage around me and throw things around my bed as I would listen to those angry words and breathe through every sensation of pain that it brought up silently.

My *guru* had instructed me: "Drop the resistance. You are the one giving meaning to those words. Hear them as pure sounds." So, I began going into a cross-legged position and consciously breathing in the pain every time that I would feel her anger. As a result, I would end up meditating 6 to 7 hours at a stretch without food, sleep, or water. One day, all the resistance that I had collapsed, and I entered the most blissful wordless state of space within myself. My mother was still angry; I could still feel her anger with closed eyes, but my inner space was tranquil and untouched. I stayed in that deep awareness for hours, witnessing hunger come and go, thirst come and go, sleep come and go, and yet this space remained untouched. It was an inner silence that my mother's harsh words could not penetrate.

The Fractals Emerge

Over the next decade, my mother and I experienced union and separation like the push and pull of the moon and the tides. Every time that I would do spiritual workshops, our connection would get better, but the love hate cycle persisted. I shifted cities, started and left jobs, and through it all, I had held back from truly opening up to her being and her essence. I had been fighting, ignoring and rebelling against what life was trying to show me through her all along. It took a long journey of intense and dedicated self-examination to peel away each of those layers. My spiritual pursuits ended in 2012 when I met a spiritual teacher who shared the teachings of Nisargadatta Maharaj, a late 19th century guru of non-duality. In one of his discussions, as recorded in the very famous book *I Am That*, I came across this dialogue:

> "**Maharaj:** In your search for love what exactly are you searching for?
>
> **Questioner:** Simply this: to love and be loved.
>
> **Maharaj:** You mean a woman?
>
> **Questioner:** Not necessarily. A friend, a teacher, a guide – as long as the feeling is bright and clear. Of course, a woman is the usual answer. But it need not be the only one.
>
> **Maharaj:** Of the two what would you prefer, to love or be loved?
>
> **Questioner:** I would rather have both! But I can see that to love is greater, nobler and deeper. To be loved is sweet, but it does not make one grow.
>
> **Maharaj:** Can you love on your own, or must you be made to love?
>
> **Questioner:** One must meet somebody lovable of course. My mother was not only not loving, she was also not lovable.
>
> **Maharaj:** What makes a person lovable? Is it not the being loved? First you love and then you look for reasons.

Questioner: It can be the other way around. You love what makes you happy.

Maharaj: But what makes you happy?

Questioner: There is no rule about it. The entire subject is highly individual and unpredictable.

Maharaj: Right. Whichever way you put it, unless you love there is no happiness. But, does love always make you happy? Is not the association of love with happiness a rather early, infantile stage? When the beloved suffers, don't you suffer too? And do you cease to love, because you suffer? Must love and happiness come and go together? Is love merely the expectation of pleasure?

Questioner: Of course not. There can be much suffering in love.

Maharaj: Then what is love? Is it not the state of being rather than a state of mind? Must you know that you love in order to love? Did you not love your mother unknowingly? Your craving for her love, for an opportunity to love her, is it not the movement of love? Is not love as much a part of you, as consciousness of being? You sought the love of your mother because you loved her.

Questioner: But she would not let me!

Maharaj: She could not stop you.

Questioner: Then, why was I unhappy all my life?

Maharaj: Because you did not go down to the very roots of your being. It is your complete ignorance of yourself, that covered up your love and happiness and made you seek for what you have never lost. Love is will, the will to share your happiness with all. Being happy – making happy – this is the rhythm of love."

As part of non-duality studies, we would allow our readings to 'settle down' in our consciousness. This extract shifted me profoundly as it settled down in mine. It debased my entire ideology of love, and it uncovered the very painful thought that I did not love my mother. I had believed this for a very long time; so, I examined my actions and their deepest sources. I stopped acting out of obligation, duty, and compulsion. Instead, I allowed actions to happen naturally and spontaneously from my whole state of being.

This started making an impact on her and everyone else. The 'love detox', i.e., separating the society's idea of love versus love as Awareness itself, started making 360-degree shifts in the lives of the people who had started coming to me for inner child healing.

The Last Mile

In 2012, I decided to give up my IT career after seven adventurous years to finally come home into her lap and rest. To be with her like the child that I was meant to be. I had finally dropped my resistance of being a receiver in the relationship. I wanted to make up for all the time I had lost in fighting her love. I wanted to go that last mile.

Synchronicities started unfolding, and my life truly started falling into place when I decided to let my guard down once and accept my role as her child. I dropped my guard and learnt to be vulnerable, allowing her to affect me deeply. I taught myself to genuinely communicate with her and removing the sense of inferiority I had always felt around her while growing up. I learnt to ask her for hugs, for my favourite food, and for her care. I learnt to open my arms and receive her ways of reciprocating. I promised her that I would dedicate the first book I ever wrote to her. She in turn opened up to me about the abuse and suffering she had suffered as a child growing up in utter poverty. She shared her deep mother wound with me. I learned to hold her as the wounded child she was, never having received comfort from anyone all her life and having to endure these pains alone. I learned to hold space for her. And we began harmoniously co-existing. I learnt the value of healthy attachment and healed the abrupt severance I had experienced with her. It transcended into us becoming soul friends, where we could talk about anything under the sun and allow the other to be. We could finally love each other and express that love without binding the other in any way. This one shift created miracles in my life. All my life I had struggled to find a career that made me feel like I belonged there. That career found me. The love of my life, my current partner, found me. I recognised my longing for her in my connection with him. I fell in love with her again thanks to him. This time for real.

As I started looking deeper into the source of my longing for her, I started seeing that, like a single brush stroke moving across time, our souls part only to come back as one only to part again. In these journeys of creation and destruction, we are always one even when we are apart. I became aware of how we journey from one life to the next, but we always carry our tribe through those lifetimes. That there are no goodbyes in the continuum of life.

Thanks to this journey with my mother, I started seeing people as portals, as placeholders, for a larger dimension of life expressing itself and the yearning to come alive. It gave me the ability to listen beyond what people were saying. Through my healing work, all I really did was connect people to the messages that were longing to come through to them from their higher space. People started to experience shifts within a single session. Sceptics, who didn't believe in the factuality of the eternal nature of connections, started receiving experiences through these sessions that crumbled their defiance and took their life in unforeseen, miraculous directions.

Just as I had realised this in my own life, those who were working with me to resolve their relationships with their parents started seeing how their connection with their mother was mirrored back to them by the universe in their connection to everything else. How, like fractals, when we shift that one story, drop that one belief that holds us back from experiencing oneness with her, their entire universe seemed to shift. It also began shifting my relationship with my body. It transformed from being a canvas of abuse into a blank tranquil space that carried profound aliveness. When I healed my birth story, it shifted me from being a sickly child, who despised any physical activity, to a person who could walk for hours, cycle 20 kilometres, and do yoga for eight straight hours.

This connection with the mother reflected into the connection with a bigger mother: the Earth. I felt connected to the Earth for the first time in my life. My diet became a conscious one. I started receiving body-based intuitions, which were visceral messages, that guided me to deeper healing modalities such as Rebirthing Breathwork and Craniosacral Therapy to heal my primal consciousness. I also began doing healing work with my entire body through Creative Movement Therapy workshops. I started receiving specific guidance related to herbs and fragrances and their effect on people's mental and emotional wellbeing. I started seeing people's past life manifestation on their bodies. That led to miraculous results. I started living an unimagined life.

The shifts didn't stop there. I began connecting to the source of the rage that used to run through me and her. It dawned on me that not all anger is a negative emotion. It opened my eyes to *sacred anger*, something well known in Zen philosophies, as the representation that our *kundalini* energy takes when its purpose is to break the momentum of the unconscious mind. I learnt to honour and respect her rage and acknowledged its source.

Though it was an internal shift within me, I could see the effect that it had on her. She never had fits of rage ever since. That's when it brought about another profound seeing. I started experiencing the feeling that I live in a world made up of mirrors. One of the ancient scriptures of India say that this world is an illusion, maybe what they truly meant was that there are 'switches' within us. Switches to all that occurs around us only we are willing to be present to the vastness of who we are. This meditative experience uprooted my foundations of blame, the most toxic force in any relationship. I realised that there was no 'other.' Whenever my childish ego wanted to resign into blame, this realisation would pull me back from deluding myself. This simple erasure of blame transformed my relationships and made them come alive.

The Gift of the Present

For several years now, our family is experiencing a new reality. My mother bought me a house to do my healing work and to have my own space. We live together at least twice or thrice a week, and it has become a joyful atmosphere brimming with life and wonders. She is cooking for me as I write this chapter. She makes sure that I am fed as I pursue my dreams single-mindedly. I realise that there are a lot of worldly things that I need to learn from her. I am touched by her devotion to us. I share my fears with her, let her hold me as I cry, share my dreams with her, and there is a non-judgmental space between us where it all flows like the effortless breeze. She has found a new person in me. She sees my flaws, but instead of being a critic, she mischievously gets me to see them. My inner parent is alive within her, and her inner child is alive within me. We alternate between feeling connected and giving space to each other. I listen to her stories of childhood, ideas of home décor, and intuitions about world economy and people. We listen to that space between us that pulses with the immensity of love. Love, not an emotion or a passing feeling, but a state of being, the nature of connection between everything in this universe.

A few months ago, we made a pilgrimage as a family. We went to her grandmother's house, a dilapidated structure where she was born. It was once a prospering harbour town built by the British. She had stopped visiting her cousins in that town after she was nine, owing to the acute shame of her abject poverty. As she took me through the streets that had almost completely changed within the last five decades, trying to locate her cousin's house, we were filming her, capturing her excitement as she travelled through time while walking through those streets. She showed us her favourite window sill that she used to love sitting on.

We felt embalmed as a family that day.

This journey has taught me several lessons: how important full circles are in life; how, in order to heal every part of us, we must travel to the roots first; and how we forge destructive beliefs using our childhood perceptions. It has also taught me to value love. And that love is an ongoing process of purification that has no end game. It has also made me aware that healing never really ends. Our minds have ways to recycle old wounds. At the end of what feels like a trip, I find myself coming home to who I innately am. The process of clearing of the layers that cover up this natural essence and of letting my true self emerge is a constant work in progress, but it has become easier. It has emptied me of my quests and has instead compelled me to look beyond. The 'hero' in me discovers new perceptions of home constantly.

Recently, I wrote a piece on my Facebook wall that summed up this state-of-being accurately.

Contentment.
I watch this mind and see the many transformations
it tells me I need to make. But this watcher I suspect
myself to be looks up and sees the sun quietly steady
on the horizon. I do nothing. There is no "I have
to overcome this" and "I have to transform this"
spiritual treadmill.

I let inner me Be.

I experience worry, stress and anxiety. My mind is
chaos. It's spinning a 100 stories a minute. And I'm
very caught up in watching it intently. And then
there is remembrance that this is not everything. I
look up. In that brief glimpse I view my unflinching
and dim, but a certain, presence. When I look
down, the chaos is still there, unaffected.

But I'm no longer the one perturbed. There is
no longing for peace. There's no desire or need for
peace. I know my inner universe is out of control.
But the one who pursued spirituality in order to
gain control is nowhere to be found.
I know now that the deepest layer of our mind
isn't love – it isn't fear or polarity either, but rather
control. Transformation-based spirituality works on
love - fear. It used to call out to me.
But transcendence 'rests' that deeper layer of me,
like an organism affected by the perception of
control.
And as I see this affected part, I start noticing how
Contentment is my most natural state. And what
an immense freedom it is to not have to transform,
overcome, create or destroy!

If you've had a difficult childhood and want to create harmony in your personal and professional relationships, Deepti is the person to go to. If you have run the treadmills of spirituality for years but haven't yet experienced transformation in your key relationships, Deepti will help you connect to that lost part in you that has remained untouched by your spiritual pursuits.

By combining both transformational and transcendental schools of spirituality and integrating them with embodied psychological practices, she gets people to the root cause of their manifested issues and helps transform them - often within a single session. She documents her experiences of integrating spirituality into ordinary life and relationships in her blog. Her blog has touched people all around the world, including Dr Christiane Northrup who is a leading Hay House author. Dr Christiane shared her blog as an example of one of the most vulnerable pieces of writing she had come across. Deepti regularly writes for India's no.1 spiritual magazine, Life Positive, as well as for Complete Wellbeing, an international publication for wellness.

Being trained in Rebirthing Breathwork and an active organiser for workshops conducted by Rebirthing Breathwork International, she was appointed the Vice President of the India Chapter by its founder, Leonard Orr. She has also been certified for Inner Child work from Life Research Academy, India, and will soon be a certified Family Constellation facilitator.

Deepti G Gujar
Website: www.creawithin.com
Facebook: https://www.facebook.com/Chriiya
Twitter: www.twitter.com/deeptiggujar
LinkedIn: https://uk.linkedin.com/in/deeptigujar

Relentless –
The Journey of
Building A Multi-Million Dollar
Business

S A I   B L A C K B Y R N

H i, I'm Sai Blackbyrn, and this chapter is about the story of my success in the world of coaching and how I got to where I am. I own and manage a multimillion dollar company, employ many individuals, and help people transform their lives. Because of my humble beginnings, I didn't have any work experience or a formal degree to rely on. So, I started the earlier versions of this business without any formal degree, without any work experiences, and without having worked in this industry as an employee; I started this before I could get any of those things. Now that I introspect, not having the experience gave me the courage to experiment as much as I did.

Being Dyslexic, but Not Limited

My life at school taught me only one thing: the only way to get anywhere is to relentlessly keep working against the tide. You see, unbeknownst to me, my school had diagnosed me with dyslexia. According to my mother's wishes, I was never told that. I only knew that what came easily to most children in my class was really, really difficult for me. Needless to say, I felt terrible in school, and I ended up dropping out of high school. By the time I quit, I had managed to learn how to catch up, though. This is not to say that I blame my mother—far from it actually.

You see, my mother is and always was my biggest champion. She believes that to acknowledge weakness is to give in. So, throughout my school years, she never allowed the school to acknowledge my dyslexia. This meant that I would never get all the support I would have gotten as a dyslexic student. As a dyslexic student, you got in special classes and you were given extra time during the exams. These things really did give you a bit of an advantage, but I never got that because my mother decided otherwise. She said, "You know what, he's going to compete with all the other regular kids."

So yes. I started to compete, unsuccessfully at first, with all the other kids who weren't dyslexic. The only thing I knew was that I had her full support. Despite the setbacks, the bad grades, and the slow growth, I persisted as she tutored me through it. As it turns out, the system was easily gamed. I had an incredible memory; with my mother's help, I figured out how I can leverage that in order to turn my Ds into straight As. Her belief in me was unwavering and strong, no matter what happened. You see, a child doesn't necessarily know she/he is different, and sometimes having that tag of 'special needs' can hurt more than help.

I decided, as I started to see the cracks in the system, not to continue my education after getting my high school diploma because I knew that it places no value on creative thought. I realised that it valued the fine details, the 'what' of it all, so much more than the 'why' and the 'how.' As a super smart kid whose only challenge was getting letters mixed up in his mind, I could see that the education system places more importance on how you write and read things instead of valuing the intent and the meaning of it.

My Mother: My Champion, My Teacher

My mother was a first-generation Indian who came here and made a life for herself in London, despite all the pushback. I was born in London but being brown in a place like London warrants a very specific type of experience. No matter what your ethnicity, if you were brown, you were labelled 'that Paki kid.' I know for sure my mother didn't want me to get more labels before I could build my own self-identity. She didn't want me to think of myself as the dyslexic kid. She didn't want me and others to give me any room for failure.

When she came over to London, she was an immigrant, a woman, and an Indian. All these things obviously carried prejudice with it, especially in those days, but she never wanted to acknowledge these labels. She was always an entrepreneur. Growing up, I always knew her as a person who built her own business, but she never wanted to be known as the immigrant woman entrepreneur. To her, she was just building things. The interesting thing was that whenever she failed, she never attributed it her being a woman or being Indian. She always had a reason that was within her control, which meant that she first had to take responsibility for those failures.

Now that I remember some of my experiences as I was growing up, it is rather funny. I remember meeting one of my mum's friends when I was building the first few projects and she was telling me about her campaign to break the glass ceiling so that women can have equal rights as men. I remember thinking that that was such a bullshit way to spend your life—where somebody is fighting a cause that is futile. You see, for me, I never experienced any of that. Not because my experience was that of a male entrepreneur, but because my mother never chose to acknowledge it. In her space, she was the master of her destiny. She was the captain of her ship, and no one could tell her that she couldn't do something because she was an Indian or she was a woman.

So, growing up with her, I never saw being Indian, being a woman, or being dyslexic as something of a disadvantage. When you saw her work, you knew that she'd break the glass ceiling simply because she didn't care enough about it. To her, it was just a minor inconvenience, like racists. They could try and tell her that her experience and achievements were going to be limited because of who she was, and she just laughed in the face of it and kept working. Women like her may not campaign for breaking the glass ceilings, but people like her are the leaders who actually break it.

As I said earlier, I didn't know that I was diagnosed with dyslexia. Later, I didn't acknowledge it as a negative thing. It was only when I was older that I realized my mother never let me acknowledge that part of my personality, and I needed to figure out how I felt about it. It was only after a lot of thinking that I understood that part of me. I remember taking the test in school as a child, but I didn't know the result because the school wasn't allowed to reveal the result to me. Apparently, the school had insisted on special classes, and she didn't want any part of that. Her kid would not be treated differently if she could help it and help it she could. So, here we are.

I did end up finishing school and earned good grades. However, in the end, I decided not to go to university. The reason behind this decision was simple: I always knew I was going to be an entrepreneur, a business owner. When I spoke to my mum and everybody else I knew about my vision, I realized that about 90% of them said that a university degree didn't do much for their entrepreneurial vision. All it did was it got them their first job. So, when they became business owners, they had to relearn their own vision, their own path. Following the university path has a way of commanding you in a very specific direction.

As I learned more about dyslexia and what special classes do to the morale of kids, I understood what my mother had done for me. She, knowing how much I could handle, had given me my greatest hill to climb when I wasn't afraid to do it. Because we never acknowledged dyslexia, it never existed in our reality; so, I had to take responsibility for my actions and be in control of my life, just like my mother was in control of hers. Not acknowledging the glass ceiling allowed her to break it; not acknowledging dyslexia allowed me to see my limitless potential. The problem with labels is that when we label people, we forgo personal responsibility for our own destiny. We blame our label for not having achieved our goals. We console ourselves that we could have achieved it if we weren't A, B, or C. My mother never let this determine her fate. If she didn't achieve something, it was because she didn't achieve it. In looking for reasons behind it, she attributed it to something she could control, and in that came power. In responsibility comes power, and that's the biggest lesson my mother has taught me: to take responsibility for my own destiny.

It is a simple thing, but even today when I'm stringing together a sentence, I struggle with the words 'you're' and 'your'. I just can't distinguish them apart or figure out how to use them because it just doesn't equate in my mind. But it never occurs to me as a limitation. It is just what it is—one of those things that confuse me. But, had I known as a child that something in my brain was not letting me see them, it wouldn't merely have been a confusing thing. It would have been a source of self-doubt and self-enforced limitations. As an adult, I know that there are bigger things than trying to figure this and that shifts the perspective for me. I know now that I can know what I know. For what I can't, I can develop or find tools. As a child, it would have impaired the growth of my confidence.

Being a Dating Coach

So, after school, I decided to start my own business and I dabbled in a lot of things until a personal interest of mine, dating, came up. I realized that there were communities of people, mostly men, who wanted to better themselves and attract others to them. What they would do is approach women everywhere in order to connect, attract and get dates almost every day. They would approach them everywhere: bars, clubs, the streets, cinemas, libraries, and just wherever they could build connections in order to get these dates. This was quite interesting to me, and I became obsessed with the art of connecting. Eventually, I got quite good at this whole art of approaching, attracting, and connecting. Eventually, I had people who asked me to teach them.

Little by little, I started to teach people how to do it, and I started charging for it as I became well known. As it turns out, one of my clients was extremely well-off. After his sessions, he told me about his wealth and how he inherited it. He told me this because he wanted to invest in my business, and he wanted to bring it out to Western

Australia. So, of course, we did. Now, the interesting thing about getting investments is that it gives you a false sense security. What I didn't understand then was that when you get an early investor while you're developing your business, they end up controlling everything. In my case, I do mean everything. I had unwittingly signed a document saying that he had full control of not only the financial parts of the business but also of the final decision making. Essentially, he could decide the full direction and scope of my business.

This investor of mine had never run a business. He didn't see the value of his money because he hadn't earned any of it. It was all just handed to him as an inheritance. This distinction matters a lot here because he didn't understand how a business grows. He didn't understand how one invests everything—blood, sweat, and tears—in order to build it. He was happy thinking that his investment alone was a fair trade of the full control that he had given himself. I didn't understand then that his lack of ownership would affect my business, and I could never have predicted the extent to which it did end up affecting it in the end.

As we were building it, I was doing all the work: giving seminars and selling packages and training programs on the back of these seminars. Pretty soon, we had turned it into Western Australia's largest dating coaching company, and this title was an enormous point of success for us. However, over time, I realized that there was a big disconnect between my vision and the vision of the investor. He and I wanted to take the company in entirely different directions, so trouble started to brew. What I started to notice was that because of that dissonance, our business was starting to suffer. So much so that our client intake started to get lower and lower. After doing all that work to be successful and get to where we were, we lost it because of differences in ideologies and broken team dynamics.

After a few months of losing our title, we decided to run a retreat in Bali. We took 15 students there in an effort to reinvigorate our brand. It was hugely successful! Not only were we able to provide transformative experiences to the students, we made a boatload of money as well, which is always awesome. As we were beginning our journey back to Australia, I was super excited to get back to work and build my brand back up to where it was and where it could go. But, just then, I hit red tape square in the face. Bureaucratic disaster hit me big time.

The Immigration Woes

As I was returning to Australia after the Bali retreat, I was stopped at immigration. They asked me all kinds of questions, but the gist of it was this: to make money in Australia from a business I was running, I needed to have a have a business visa. I thought I had it, but as it turns out, my exploratory business visa didn't allow me to run the business the way a regular business visa would. I wasn't allowed to earn money from my business. Because I wasn't allowed to do that, I had invalidated the terms of my visa by doing earning money. I was essentially not allowed to return to Australia.

The authorities took me inside a room. It was surrounded by mirrors and had a tiny desk and two stools. They interrogated me for about three hours. I was asked almost every imaginable question: what was I doing in Australia, why was I there, what did I bring to the country, and more. In the end, I was asked to write an exam. I was supposed to write why I should be let back and kept in the country. That was it. My entire future and the future of my company depended on how well I answered one single question!

They gave me this question, but I didn't really understand what they wanted, so I did my best to give the answers I thought they wanted. I told them about my business, about how I was a job creator, how we provided educational opportunities, and other things I thought they wanted to hear. I wrote three pages about my worth to the country. They returned, took the paper away, and left me there by myself for about thirty minutes.

As I waited, I thought how funny this story is going to be. I kept thinking how this was going to be the story of how I was 'almost' kicked out of Australia. I was relaxed, and I was fully prepared as a dating coach to charm my immigration officer into letting me fix the bureaucratic error. What I wasn't prepared for was the results of the exam. My immigration officer returned with a poker face, and I saw her lips move. She said, "Sai, according to the immigration act 111b, we have decided to revoke your visa and place a 3-year ban on you entering the country, effective immediately." As she said that, I realized that I was locked out and stuck with just a handful of belongings. I had a few clothes, my laptop, a microphone, and $300. My bank accounts were frozen, and everything that I had in Australia was just gone. Poof! All in a single moment.

They put me in a detention centre and deported me to Bali the very next day. Now, I understand it when you take a second to scoff. Everybody says the same thing, "Sai, you are exaggerating mate, there are definitely worse places to be deported back to", but nobody factors in my meagre possessions. I had 300 bucks, my bank accounts were frozen, and I had nowhere to stay. Above that, I only had a 30-day visa for Bali. With these limitations, I knew I had to figure out a plan pretty quickly or I was going to be in trouble because the detention centre in Indonesia was going to be way worse than that in Australia. You see, the detention centre in Indonesia is exactly what it sounds like: a place where the authorities detain you. The Australian detention centre, on the other hand, was like a very well-protected boarding school. They had all the amenities you could want. I had access to everything as I waited: play stations, games, Internet, books, food, and just about everything. So, you see, I was justifiably worried.

Exiled

At this point in time, my investor cut me off completely. He said that he was only going to fund the business if I could figure out a way to make it work online. So, I was stuck in Bali and didn't have enough money for a ticket to London. In hindsight, I know that if I really wanted to, I could have begged and borrowed a few tenners from my Facebook friends and gone back, but I didn't really want to. What was I going back to? I had no money, no work experience, and no degree. In London, the only 'job' I had done was that of a waiter. All I had ever seen success in was being an entrepreneur. Even if I went back, the only thing I would be doing is running back to the familiar and the comfortable. I had no prospects in London. I decided that it would be easier to try and make it in Bali. And boy, am I glad that I did! I know for a fact that had I gone back to England, had I had a university degree to fall back on, I would not be as successful as I am now. I would have never owned my own business.

So, I stayed and tried to figure out how to get the 'Internet to work' for me. I started looking at my Facebook friends and thought about the people I knew, trying to find somebody who knew how to do internet marketing. I was trying to find someone who was already successful at it, and luckily, I found Adam Davis. I reached out to him, telling him how I was trying to create an online program, but I didn't know how to do it and sell it. He started to mentor me, and over the course of a month, he taught me how to build a program and sell it. At the end of the month, I was even starting to see the results. He taught me about the concept of an online funnel, about directing clients through the funnel and converting them into paying clients. It was starting to work, too. I had started to get a few clients through it. This meant that I could pay to extend my visa in Bali for another 30 days, which was great. I was finally starting to see the light at the end of the tunnel.

Slowly but surely with the help of Adam's mentorship, I started to succeed. I started to generated cash flow again. Our dating business, which was originally a seminar-based business, had successfully become an online business. Now here is where my naivety came back into play. My investor, despite his earlier claim, decided to use a loophole within our contract to not pay me for any of this work. In a bid to reclaim his money, he kept all the funds and ignored all the work that I had done to transform the business. I ended up losing my share of the profit, and what I got was just enough to pay for my visa extension. Now, this is where I started to panic because not only was my rent due in a few days, he even owned my entire business concept, the intellectual property. Even if I decided not to work for him, I could not use any of the business plans I had developed for that business because he owned it. So, unless I could somehow build a new business from scratch, I could not survive.

Sink or Swim

Now, it is interesting that when we are threatened with a make or break moment, we do make it. In times of sink or swim, we humans swim. I started thinking about the skills that I did have, skills that no one could claim as part of any intellectual property. I had managed to build this business into Western Australia's largest dating coaching business, and then I had successfully moved my business online. Surely I wasn't the only coach who had struggled with building their coaching business. Surely there were others who were struggling to do what I had done. So, I reached to all my old contacts, people who had seen our meteoric rise and had wanted to learn how to do it.

I offered them a simple deal: I'll offer my services for free, and my fee is only due if I succeed. I had to offer this deal because I really had no other reference point of success. I still remember my first client, Jan, who hired me. Jan turned ordinary people into extraordinary artists simply by rewiring their neural associative conditioning. Her clients went from drawing stick figures to amazing art, and the irony is that Jan can't draw at all. All she knew was how to rewire the brain. Anyway, the problem Jan had was that she was struggling to fill up her seminars. She did not know how to market it at all. So, I started applying the same strategies that I used to use to fill up our seminars, which was mostly Facebook ads. Pretty soon, she had fully booked seminars, three months in advance. Her coaching business went from being undersubscribed to being oversubscribed.

Another notable client I had was Roberto. Roberto was a happiness coach, and he essentially taught people how to be happy. As I was looking at his business from the marketing angle, it wasn't a powerful niche. I started to work with him to refine that. As it turns out, Roberto was a great golfer, and he had taught himself how to be a great golfer using neurolinguistic programming. This was it! I could see how this could be his niche. We worked with him to produce a business around that: how to become an amazing golfer using the inner game of golf. Within 48 hours of us launching that program, he had over 40 applications, all requesting to work with him one-on-one. Again, massively oversubscribed.

By this time, word of these successes was spreading fast in Bali. As it happens, a celebrity coach was living in Bali at the same time I was there. He was watching me succeed with absolute fascination. After Jan and Roberto's success, he approached me and told me that he wanted to launch a new product and wanted my help to launch it as he was a good public speaker but not an online guy. He, Chris, had negligible presence online. So, we decided to custom build a funnel for his business, and as we were doing that, I was starting to become financially solvent because of all the wins I've had so far with my clients. I also understood that doing this work for Chris would change the level of my business. If I could make him succeed, I knew that he would give me the best testimonial ever and introduce me to a ton of people and essentially change the scope of my business. I could see that with his recommendation, this business could even become bigger than the dating coaching business in Australia, so I worked relentlessly to make this launch go off without a hitch.

Dot Coach Is Born

On the day of the launch, we had positioned everything to make sure that he would get an abundant amount of sales right off the bat. We thought we were ready and prepared. Turns out you can never prepare yourself for ground-breaking success. I was floored! You see, as we were building up to the launch, I had known it would do well, but I couldn't imagine the scope of it, the sheer flood of money. I knew that I was good at what I did, and that it was a good plan, but even I could not have predicted the level of success that we achieved. With the sheer success of this program, I could finally see my future. I could see the behemoth that I could build. I was finally doing amazing things, and this time I had no shady investor. I finally owned my own success.

I know that over the course of the lifetime of that funnel, it generated thousands of clients, hundreds of thousands of dollars, and thousands of upsells. Of course, that made our celebrity coach, Chris, very happy. He gave us the glowing testimonial, he introduced me to his networks, and he offered to promote us on several occasions. This, this was the moment that my business Sai.coach was born. Dot coach was finally my own.

Yes, we still had failures and we still had things that didn't work. However, projects that did work did wildly well. Our biggest programs made an insane amount of money for us with ridiculous profit margins, and I was finally able to think about more than rent.

Five years later, we have a staff of 34 people, we have clients in 43 countries, we have 3.6 million fans on Facebook, and we've created a multimillion-dollar business out of a forced exile, 300 dollars, a computer, a microphone, and an iron will. I personally love our story, because our business is based on transformations. It is a business based on making a difference in other people's lives.

If I were to derive lessons out of this journey and offer my advice, I would start with these things:

Get a Mentor

When you are starting any new journey, get a mentor. Notice that I said mentor and not a coach. A coach is somebody who is ideally certified to help and thinks that they can help. A mentor is somebody who has been exactly where you are and has taken the journey you are about to. They have been exactly where you want to be. By taking a mentor's advice and following it through and being accountable, you can shorten your journey by not months or even 1–2 years, but by even decades! A mentor can give you their experience. By approaching Adam Davis, my mentor, when I did, I was able to cut short my journey by years. He was able to guide my journey in a far straighter line than I could ever have. He saved me the time I would have spent understanding minor things.

I see so many people doing so many things without a mentor. I see them go zig zag, forwards and then backwards again, and they never get anywhere. A mentor can shortcut that journey by incredible amounts.

Flip the Coin

No matter who you are, no matter what discrimination you face, there is going to be someplace where you could make a difference. As a young person of Indian descent, I faced discrimination in London, but oddly enough, it has only ever helped me in my industry. Lucky for me, India is the original land of coaching with gurus paving the way for my industry. Indian professionals have also built a good reputation as tech experts. So, as a young Indian, my ethnic background, my cultural history, and the international reputation of people who look like me—all of it—has allowed me to be seen favourably in my industry. So, stick to it and find a way to flip the perspective.

Be Relentless!

When it comes to starting a business, being relentless is the only way to do it. Being relentless is one of the most important things you'll ever do for your business. As I look back at my school years, I can see the paths all my peers took, and the divide between the groups amazes me. I can clearly see that the C students, the dyslexics, and the marginalized are the ones who ended up creating and running companies that the A students will work in. The A students became good employees, but ironically, they were only ever working for the companies that the C students had built. It really confused me, because growing up I thought that if anybody was happy and successful, it's the A students. You know, the people who had it easy and those that just had to show up and excel at everything.

I kept thinking about the commonality of this flipping of roles, and then it finally came to me. I had to constantly overcome adversity right from the get-go by having to deal with my own limitations and constantly getting up again when life threw me down. All of this prepared me for the business world. My relentlessness was my biggest strength. People like me succeed because we have to. We have no other choice. All we know is getting back up.

People who were smart, people who had it really easy in school and life, burn out fast when life throws adversity at them. They had no idea how to deal with failure. They didn't know how to get up again. We, the side-lined ones, are great at standing tall and getting up again. In the world of business, when you are approaching, connecting and building something precious, you have to fail constantly and keep trying.

So, go ahead: Fail. Fail hard and get up again. Forget about dignity and poise and all of those words that people use when they are trying to make you feel bad about being relentless in your struggles. Get up, and pick others up. Mentor and be mentored.

S ai Blackbyrn is an entrepreneur, a coach, a mentor, a father, a husband, and a CEO. He started working towards his vision right out of high school, and his charm and natural understanding of human behaviour allowed him to build Western Australia's biggest dating coaching company.

As a young entrepreneur facing immigration problems, he's learned how to set up a foolproof online business that can be sustained from anywhere, no matter what. Sai has failed over and over till he's mastered the recipe for success in the field of coaching, and he can help you build your business. You can reach out to him for a coveted seat in his FREE webinar, and learn how he helps his clients scale up fast to a 6 figure income.

He helps clients set up a foolproof operation where the clients come to them — all ready for the process to start. Sai believes in fighting relentlessly for things he's invested in, so why not get him fighting for you and your growth?

Please contact Sai at sai@sai.caoch

36691190R00121

Printed in Great Britain
by Amazon